The Historical Jesus
Goes to Church

The Historical Jesus
Goes to Church

Roy W. Hoover
Stephen J. Patterson
Lane C. McGaughy
Joe Bessler-Northcutt
Hal Taussig
Glenna S. Jackson
Charles W. Hedrick
Francis Macnab

with an introduction by Arthur J. Dewey

The Historical Jesus Goes to Church

Published in 2004 by Polebridge Press, P.O. Box 6144, Santa Rosa, California 95406.

ISBN 0-944344-61-5

Library of Congress Cataloging-in-Publication Data

The historical Jesus goes to church // [contributors, Joe Bessler-Northcutt ... et al.].
    p. cm.
  Includes bibliographical references.
  ISBN 0-944344-61-5
  1. Jesus Christ–Historicity. 2. Church. I. Bessler-Northcutt, Joe.

BT303.2.H484 2004
232.9'08–dc22

2004044442

Table of Contents

Introduction 1
Arthur J. Dewey

The Art of Gaining and Losing Everything 11
Roy W. Hoover

If You Give a Mouse a Cookie . . . What the
Quest Holds in Store for the Church 31
Stephen J. Patterson

American Churches & The Culture Wars 43
Lane C. McGaughy

Learning to See God — Prayer and Practice
in the Wake of the Jesus Seminar. 51
Joe Bessler-Northcutt

The Contemporary American Search for
Community & the Historical Jesus. 65
Hal Taussig

The Jesus Seminar in Africa 81
Glenna S. Jackson

The "Good News" about the Historical Jesus. 91
Charles W. Hedrick

Preaching the New Faith 105
Francis Macnab

Notes 123

Works Consulted. 132

Contributors

Joe Bessler-Northcutt is Associate Professor of Theology at Phillips Theological Seminary in Tulsa, Oklahoma. His book *Jesus: A Scandalous Theology* is forthcoming.

Arthur J. Dewey is Professor of Theology, Xavier University, Cincinnati, Ohio. He is the author of *Spirit and Letter in Paul* (1996) and *The Cologne Mani Codex* (with Ron Cameron, 1978).

Charles W. Hedrick is Distinguished Professor of Religious Studies at Southwest Missouri State University. His books include *The Gospel of the Savior* (with Paul Mirecki, 1999), *When History and Faith Collide* (1999), and *Parables as Poetic Fictions* (1994).

Roy W. Hoover is Weyerhaeuser Professor of Biblical Literature and Professor of Religion Emeritus, Whitman College. He is co-author (with Robert W. Funk) of *The Five Gospels* (1993) and editor of *Profiles of Jesus* (2003).

Glenna S. Jackson is Associate Professor, Department of Religion and Philosophy, Otterbein College, Westerville, Ohio. She is the author of *"Have Mercy On Me": The Story of the Canaanite Woman in Matthew 15.21-28* (2002).

Francis Macnab is Executive Minister of St Michael's Uniting Church, Melbourne, Australia, Executive Director of the Cairnmillar Institute, Melbourne, and co-founder of the Australian Foundation for Aftermath Reactions in 1990, and the author of twenty-two books.

Lane McGaughy is the Geo. H. Atkinson Professor of Religious and Ethical Studies at Willamette University, Salem, Oregon. He is the author of a *Workbook for a Beginning-Intermediate Grammar of Hellenistic Greek* (1976).

Stephen J. Patterson is Professor of New Testament at Eden Theological Seminary in St. Louis.. He is the author of several books including *The God of Jesus* (1998) and *The Gospel of Thomas and Jesus* (1993)

Hal Taussig is Visiting Professor of New Testament at Union Theological Seminary in New York, and a faculty member at Chestnut Hill College and the Reconstructionist Rabbinical College in Philadelphia. His books include *Re-imagining Life Together in America* (2002) and *Jesus Before God* (1999).

Introduction

Arthur J. Dewey

In March of this year the Jesus Seminar turned the tables around. For years associates of the Seminar had challenged the fellows to bring the historical Jesus to church. They wanted the fellows to grapple with the nitty-gritty issues of human life. But the fellows realized that the conversation was hardly one way. Many of the fellows presenting Jesus Seminars on the Road had detected how people throughout North America were struggling honestly and courageously with the question of the historical Jesus.

Many things were already underway. Religious educators Cheryl Gibbs Binkley and Jane Mitchell McKeel, for example, had completed work on an interdenominational curriculum for the fourth through the seventh grades based on the life and teaching of Jesus (*Jesus and His Kingdom of Equals*). John Butcher stitched together *An Uncommon Lectionary*. A number of pastors throughout North America took the chance and began to speak of the historical Jesus from the pulpit. Others incorporated the *Complete Gospels* into the weekly liturgies.

The fellows decided it was time to honor all those laboring in the vineyards by inviting a variety of church leaders, pastors, and associates to a seminar that would allow them a forum to share their experiences. Church leaders and their associates presented startling evidence that the historical Jesus helped people make sense of their lives together. The meeting featured examples of liturgy and preaching, prayer, education, and community action. Stories of the aching origins of some communities animated the days spent together. Communities from Tulsa to Miami, from Long Beach to Sheffield, England, from Reno to Melbourne, Australia, from different denominations, surprised one another with their insights and questions.

At the same time the fellows of the Seminar offered their critical reflections on the subject. What resulted in this critical give-and-take was a rehearsal of the future, a mini council of the churches, where wisdom and dialogue were the watchwords.

This volume is but one part of the record. For those interested in obtaining video or audio records of the meeting please contact Westar Institute at westarinstitute.org. Much of what ensued cannot be transmitted by emotionless transcript. What does follow is a collection of the papers of the fellows along with the invited presentation of Francis Macnab who, in delivering a practical demonstration of preaching the "historical Jesus," suggests some of the creative ferment of the meeting. In these papers we see the fellows struggling with the public dimension of historical-Jesus research. Each paper in its own way gives new angles on this burgeoning discussion. Each furnishes critical tools and a vocabulary for deepening the public debate. With the exception of Macnab's paper all the essays run in the order of presentation during the seminar.

In the first essay, "The Art of Gaining and Losing Everything," Roy W. Hoover clearly articulates the task facing the churches in the modern world. Can the churches see that the future of religious life lies not in providing sanctuary for the tradition against the assaults of the modern age but in meeting head-on the radical challenges of this world? Do those, who would drown out the modern world by intoning stubborn refrains of tradition, not understand that they are actually playing taps at its funeral?

Hoover declares that the radical question of gain and loss of religious meaning has been at the heart of the matter right from the beginning. Jesus of Nazareth salted his speech with the paradox of how one could lose all by attempting to hang on to things as well as gaining life through letting go. Jesus lost his life taking a risk on the reign of God. His followers began to understand even the meaning of his liquidation as a dramatic turning point. Moreover, that upright Pharisee, Paul, risked everything he was on a new understanding of what God offered the world. He abandoned what the first century deemed essential: the need for ethnic credentials to be valued as truly human.

Epochal shifts in understanding from Galileo to Darwin have brought the churches to the breaking point. Can they find the wisdom and courage to embrace the knowledge of the modern world? Can they detect its gain despite the loss of venerable forms of faith? The Jesus

Seminar from the outset has attempted to respond to this modern challenge. By using modern investigative tools the Seminar has reported on a Jesus who stood on his own two feet, not a post-mortem figment, nor a creedal collage. Hoover declares that it is time for plain speaking, rather than the legerdemain practiced by religionists who would smooth over the critical differences. He would have us admit that the Nicene Christ no longer speaks to the world. Instead, a critical understanding of Jesus' vision of the rule of God may provide us today with the basis for responsible reflection and action. He challenges the churches to lead the way in new forms of education and worship. Hoover re-envisions the very status of the Bible in the church. Scripture becomes for him the primary source of information, about the human origins of the tradition, not the magical launching pad of religious escapism.

Hoover leaves us with a fundamental challenge: what would happen if our churches actually "reflect[ed] the reality of the world as we know it and humanity's place in it?"

What would happen if our religious traditions found a human voice and assisted us in negotiating our way through this universe?

In Stephen J. Patterson's engaging essay "If You Give a Mouse a Cookie: What the Quest Holds in Store for the Church" we hear a report on what happens when Bible readers begin to discuss the historical Jesus. What happens to churches when the material of the Jesus Seminar is introduced? Patterson contends that surprising consequences follow from that first, critical step. He has discovered that three major questions surface as this conversation heats up.

Once people realize that Jesus was not just as he is treated in the Bible, then they wonder: how trustworthy is the Bible? Soon the unexamined biblical literalism shatters when the modern readers admit that they do not inhabit the landscape of the ancient cosmos. Further questions continue this unraveling. What about Scripture's inspiration and authority? What happens when "truth" and "history" are not identical? What are they to make of reports that the early Jesus believers experienced the Spirit in communal activities and not in the activity of writing? The historical observation that biblical texts have acquired value and authority, not because of inspiration or inerrancy, but because of their usefulness in cultivating faith, can prove quite unnerving.

A second wave of questions rises from considering the historical Jesus. Do not the miracles prove Jesus to be God's Son? Do we not come in contact with evidence of God's power? These uncritical questions mask an even deeper problem, namely, the omnipotence of God. If God has exhibited such power through Jesus, why in those instances and not oth-

Ehrmann

* ers? Moreover, why does the nagging reality of suffering constantly creep in? Sensitive readers notice that the complaint of Job was not answered by the rhetoric of Augustine. Indeed, the modern atmosphere, where things are truly random, violent and chaotic, dissolves any nostalgic reading of the Bible.

Patterson points out that some Bible readers continue courageously forward with their questioning. If the Bible is not history, and if Jesus' miracles are not believable, then why be concerned with Jesus at all? With what are the churches left? For Patterson the readers have what the early followers had to go on—the words and deeds of Jesus. From those fragments the early communities built a movement no one anticipated. The churches today have a choice: maintain their religious rigor mortis, stay numb to any critical questions, or move into uncharted territory by taking seriously some words that will cost them everything.

Conservative groups within and outside of mainline American churches have often criticized the Jesus Seminar, among other liberal movements. Pastors and laity alike have often avoided raising critical questions about the historical Jesus. Lane C. McGaughy provocatively subverts the common wisdom of today's churches by investigating the origins and political consequences of American denominationalism in his riveting essay "American Churches and the Culture Wars." He finds that the conservative reaction to the reports of the Jesus Seminar exemplifies a much larger historical trend that has its origin at the birth of this country.

The ratification of the Constitution created an identity crisis for religion in this country. While guaranteeing religious freedom, the establishment clause of the First Amendment prevented churches in America from enjoying state sponsorship or experiencing official persecution. If these religious groups could not be defined as established churches or outlawed sects, then what were they? Lyman Beecher provided a new category—denomination—to denote the churches as voluntary associations that could transform society. McGaughy writes that to sustain their growth and mission the denominations hit upon a two-pronged strategy: revivalism and social involvement. Later fundamentalist and liberal groups derive in part from this division of church labor.

Precisely because they were not automatically supported by the state, denominations took on the task of becoming lobbyists for their own cause, in effect, political action committees. There seemed to be no problem in this, since for many years "American civil religion" shared a common reservoir of meaning, a cultural discourse based on the Bible. But by the 1890s the increasingly pluralistic culture forced a polarization of groups in

America with the denominations deciding to push more forcefully for their ideological agenda.

More recently this partisan process turned inward as dissident groups campaigned to seize control of the churches. The very notion created by Beecher to save the churches was turned into consuming the denominations themselves. Competing moral visions of conservatives and liberals dominate much of the ecclesiastical discussions today. Indeed, many church leaders quickly give in to the demands of conservatives because they assume it is the only way to save the church. McGaughy argues that this is a major mistake. The mainline churches are forgetful of the large numbers of literate Americans, educated in universities since World War II and disinclined to follow a fundamentalist path. He wisely recommends that the churches engage directly in serious critical study of the Bible, thereby furnishing their members with the critical tools to meet the fundamentalist challenge as well as to continue the original tasks of social justice and environmental preservation. In demonstrating the value of historical research by getting to the origins and possibilities of denominationalism in America, McGaughy provides a template for bringing historical issues to the table of critical religious discourse.

D.   Joe Bessler-Northcutt leads the discussion to a creative moment. In his essay "Learning to See God: Prayer and Practice in the Wake of the Jesus Seminar" Bessler-Northcutt argues that the Jesus Seminar's findings about the historical Jesus have major christological implications. The traditional obsession with Jesus' metaphysical identity prevents the churches from realizing that a fundamental shift has occurred in understanding the significance of Jesus. The critical conclusion that the historical Jesus did not have divine pretensions, nor made himself the focus of his speech, brings Bessler-Northcutt to a radical insight. By carefully observing how the historical Jesus crafted his speech about the Empire of God, Bessler-Northcutt throws the christological discussion into an entirely new direction. Christology illuminates the social dynamics, which Jesus intimates in his speech of the Empire of God. The historical Jesus urged his audiences to imagine a social space where God's presence and not Rome's was fully established. Expendables of that Mediterranean peasant culture now had an opportunity to reframe their sense of worth and responsibility. They could gain some breathing room and a healthy skepticism of their own assumptions about the Roman-dominated world.

In considering some instances of Jesus' speech, Bessler-Northcutt discovers the basis for a creative skepticism. The parables and sayings of Jesus point to the presence of God where one least expects it—"directly in sight, under one's nose"—in the midst of human desire. It is precisely out

"Transcendence"

of this skeptical perspective that Bessler-Northcutt sees the possibility of authentic prayer in the modern world. Rejecting Christianity's traditional theistic language of God, Bessler-Northcutt relocates the primary experience of transcendence "in the midst of public life." He challenges the churches to rethink the focus of their concern. No longer can the truth-claims of the church deliver the presence of God; rather the practices of justice and compassion in public life serve as opportunities to be surprised where we least expect it.

But what happens to the churches when people begin "to see God differently," when they work to build more just and compassionate communities? They discover the original meaning of *liturgy*—the "practice of the people." Churches provide the social space where hospitality, respect, dialogue, and compassion can be practiced in a public way. People can practice the "sacrament of attentive listening" where human depths are discovered and transcendence is caught out of the corner of the eye.

In his dual role of scholar-pastor Hal Taussig deeply nuances the conversation through his essay on "The Contemporary American Search for Community and the Historical Jesus." Starting from an appraisal of contemporary American life, Taussig not only makes the case for the "American disaster of over-individualization and lack of community" but also argues that American churches are "strategically located" to help build genuine community. In contrast to the surrounding fragmentation of America, religious communities present the most likely loci to learn social repertoires and practice the habits of life together. Religious communities can become crucibles of concern as members encourage one another to think boldly about the issues that affect society as a whole.

In light of these pressing contemporary concerns, Taussig examines how the early Christian witnesses can aid the discussion. He finds in the letters of Paul the earliest complete testimony of Christian life together. In those letters teeming with the "messy negotiations about the groups' social dynamics" Taussig discerns that transcendence was inseparable from the dynamics of the particular communities. "God in Christ" was detected not in the heavens but in eyes of those around the table of fellowship. Paul was constantly burdened and braced by the character and quality of the community's life together. Neither Paul nor the communities could speak in abstract terms about God. Taussig also notes that these early communities did not emerge in a social vacuum. They drew on the various trends and models of voluntary associations and synagogues. He further wisely adds that the modern religious hope for a streamlined solution, the penchant to discover one magical model for imitation, breaks up over the complexity of the historical evidence suggesting a plurality of first-century experiences. Indeed, by making critical demands on modern interpreters, the multiplicity of models forces an honest appreciation and nuanced appropriation of the ancient material.

As he assesses the results of the voting of the Jesus Seminar Taussig notes the ambiguity of the report in regard to the question as to whether Jesus himself participated in community. The votes tended to cluster around the view that Jesus as an iconoclastic sage. There were no red or pink votes for actions of Jesus that brought people together. Yet the very teaching of Jesus was a social act that would have been embedded in the settings of meal and marketplace. Sayings about the "Empire of God" indicate an imagination quite aware of the social dilemmas of the first century. Yet Taussig finds no delineated game plan upon which to erect a unified program. In fact, he is quite aware of the "enormous mistakes and massive violence" perpetrated on people in the name of Jesus. Taussig judiciously points out that the very study of the authentic sayings of Jesus can be the occasion for shaping, reforming, and renewing community. At the same time modern interpreters are advised that these sayings are only the first step. The demands of the twenty-first century require bold advances of imagination in the quest for communal meaning. Taussig illustrates these points as he moves through various aspects of community life. He notes that the study of the historical Jesus seems to make sense to churchgoers over forty-five with substantial understanding of the tradition. On the other hand, those under thirty-five, many with little sense of history, are hardly interested. From children's formation to worship, from adult education to pastoral counseling, from outreach to preaching, Taussig makes the case that no heavy-handed use of the historical Jesus material is beneficial. Yet serious community building needs the historical Jesus as part of a critical and abundant repertoire of life.

Glenna S. Jackson explores the relevance of the historical Jesus beyond its first-world orbit in her report "The Jesus Seminar in Africa." Her moving account brings the reader to the very interface of cultures. Jackson finds that westerners can learn much from an African reading of Bible. While the Bible is quite likely the most widely read book in Africa, there are a variety of ways in which the Bible is used. Sometimes the Bible becomes a protective object, a symbol of divine presence. At other times it serves as a practical tract, providing comfort, instruction, or exhortation. Frequently the Bible becomes a matter of the heart, as African spiritualism trumps rationality. Then there are moments when the narrative defies African experience and requires an explanation. Lastly, the religious and cultural context of the Bible bears a striking resemblance to the world of contemporary Africa.

Before westerners too cavalierly bring up the question of the historical Jesus, Africans will remind their interlocutors that the original quest
for the historical Jesus was undertaken at the same time as the European
quest for African land. Indeed, this new quest for the historical Jesus
comes out of a country that would usher in a Pax Americana. Is there
more to the historical Jesus than the voiceprints of "ugly Americans"?

Jackson artfully demonstrates that the quest for the historical Jesus
has transcultural possibilities by showing how her students appropriated
and understood the parables of Jesus. They did not have to go back two
thousand years to understand the social world of the parables. Their
African context put them on familiar terms with passages that westerners
find quite distant. At the same time, by engaging her students in a critical
dialogue on the evidence for the historical Jesus, Jackson challenged the
residues of fundamentalist western missionaries in the students' imaginations. The critical discussion brought her students to a new point. By writing their own parables and stories in connection with the sayings of Jesus,
the students began to realize that they had something unique to offer to
the critical discussion. They got to the very heart of the sayings of the
historical Jesus and saw the possibilities of a changed world in their midst.

Despite the numerous critics who think that the work of the Jesus
Seminar has undermined "faith," sowed doubt, and performed a major disservice to the churches, Charles W. Hedrick argues for "The 'Good News'
about the Historical Jesus." He contends that a critical study of the past
becomes "good news" when it causes us to grow by modifying our perspectives and behaviors. The investigation into the historical Jesus makes a
significant contribution to the future of the church by coming to grips
with its very origins. Hedrick points out that scholarly research into the
origins of the church has demonstrated that the Jesus of contemporary
Christian orthodoxy is an early second-century construct formulated from
inferences on the early Christian tradition. Even the kerygma and rudi-
mentary creeds of the first century were mythic constructions that omit
the very words and deeds of Jesus.

Hedrick clearly points out that the "historical Jesus" determined by
historians is not really a construct but "a disassociated collection of raw
data." This material offers the church an opportunity to reconstitute itself
and its message for the twenty-first century. For the first time since the
second century the church has the chance to draw its own inferences
about Jesus. Such a task is essential since the Enlightenment and modern
sciences have undermined the mythic formulations that have long been
in use. Will the people decide that they can no longer live a schizophrenic
 existence? How long will the churches continue to shore up the outdated

mythic superstructure? Could it be that, once the mythic construct has been removed, there is nothing left of faith?

Hedrick reminds the reader that this reevaluation is not novel. For some early communities the death of Jesus provoked a variety of attempts to make sense of his end. Nevertheless, other communities, like Q and Thomas, stressed his words of life and wisdom. With the arrival of the creedal formulations the raw material of Jesus' words and deeds fell out of the ecclesiastical equation. In each case the communities sought "something more" that would provide the basis for ethical behavior. They went beyond the "data" to construct models for life together. Hedrick ends with a challenge to the modern church: can we take up the fragments of the historical Jesus dislodged by historical analysis and draw new inferences from that data? Can the church learn from its complicated past and refashion itself for the future?

The final paper delivers the work of a lifetime. Francis Macnab, pastor and therapist, theologian and poet, presents a stunning illustration of "Preaching the New Faith." In his introductory remarks he acknowledges that he has already outgrown a God who desires blood and body bags. He has little sympathy for any religious tradition that consigns the human spirit to the little ease of despair. Our churches have remained stuck in the holding patterns of the past, unable to provide a clue to the new context of the modern world. Now is time to "crack the code"! It is time to stay true to the hints of humanity in our experience; time to acknowledge that the God of conventional religion is long gone; time to leave behind the abusive demands still muttering in our lives.

Macnab brings forward the wisdom of the historical Jesus for our consideration. He finds that Jesus pointed to the surprising presence of God. The God of Jesus provides the glue, the tissue of trust in our lives. In the very midst of life Jesus intimated the enchantment of God. If we would but look up, at one another, and allow the explosion of abundance to go off in our hearts, what would our universe look like?

In the final part of his presentation Macnab takes the listener on a poetic procession through the worship service at St. Michael's Uniting Church. His personal marginalia and recasting of traditional texts demonstrate the creative forces at work at St. Michael's. The reminiscence of his revision of the Lord's Prayer for a dying man will leave no reader unmoved. Through Macnab's words the code seems to crack, perhaps for a moment, as we glimpse "the goodness that flows from the heart of the universe."

The Art of Gaining
& Losing Everything

Roy W. Hoover

Introduction: Russian Believers and Bach as Theologian

In the Fall of 1992 a group of American religious educators, of whom I was one, visited three cities in the former Soviet Union—Moscow, Tashkent, and St. Petersburg—to meet religious leaders and to learn about the resurgence of religion in a land that had until recently been ruled by a political regime that was ideologically committed to atheism. In a discussion about their curriculum with the dean and several faculty members at the St. Petersburg School of Theology, a Russian Orthodox institution, I asked whether they made use of historical-critical method in their courses on the Bible. "No," the dean replied; "we want our students to become believers, not philosophers."

The dean's theory of theological education, it seems, was that if you wanted to be a person of faith, you had to turn your back on the modern world, intellectually, and take up residence in the ancient world of the Bible and the world of premodern religious tradition. That one might find a way to locate one's religious life and understanding in the same modern world where one actually lived was apparently considered to be unlikely, perhaps even impossible. For the dean and his colleagues, embracing the modern world risks losing everything and gains nothing of value.

The Russian dean's expression of discomfort with the methods of modern biblical scholarship was dramatic in its forthrightness, but scarcely unique. Even among some prominent American representatives of such scholarship there is unease about its effect upon familiar realms of faith and meaning. In a recently published collection of essays that span five decades of his work as a scholar and teacher, Paul Minear, a renowned Yale Divinity School professor, now emeritus, considers the disparate worlds of ancient biblical authors and modern biblical scholars and laments the loss of theological meaning in so much of modern religious scholars'work.[1] An early storm warning was raised about the conflict between modern historical scholarship and traditional forms of religious meaning, he suggests, in the spirited contest that erupted at St. Thomas School in Leipzig between the now celebrated cantor, Johann Sebastian Bach, and a brilliant young philologist, Johann August Ernesti, who had been appointed the new rector [headmaster] at the school. Ernesti's slender volume, *Elementary Principles of Interpretation,* first published in 1761, came to be regarded as "a landmark in biblical studies"[2] both in Germany and in America. Ernesti proposed that "the Scriptures are to be investigated by the same rule as other books" and that the first aim of biblical interpretation is to discern in the text "the same meaning that the author himself attached to it."[3] In advocating this view Ernesti exhibited the spirit of the eighteenth-century Enlightenment with its interest in philological evidence and historical meaning. Bach, on the other hand, "was a devout, zealous Lutheran who continued the spirit, ethos, and biblical understanding of the seventeenth century."[4] In his music Bach aimed not to capture the meaning a text held for its original author, but to convey the events narrated in the text to "the contemporary audience whose members are called on to respond to those events in unqualified immediacy and with their whole being."[5] For Bach the Bible was to be treated *differently* from other books, because *God,* not merely a human author, speaks through the Bible . Minear thinks Bach was a better exegete than Ernesti, because Bach aimed to convey to his hearers the religious power and meaning affirmed in the scriptural texts of his chorales and cantatas, whereas Ernesti's aim was only to discern what the texts had meant to their authors.

Professor Minear has a point in claiming that an interpretation of scripture that pays attention to the religious meaning it conveys is more adequate than one which considers only its linguistic features and historical circumstance. Nevertheless, there is an instructive irony to note in the fact that not even the splendor of Bach's musical genius has been able to preserve the premodern religious meaning with which Bach wanted to impress and captivate his audience. In another recent study of Bach as a theologian the author ruefully notes that whereas seventy-five percent of

Bach's more than one thousand compositions were intended for perform-
ance in church, seventy-five percent of what we hear today in concert
halls and broadcasts are from the twenty-five percent of Bach's nonreligious works. It is undeniable, he says, "that most of those who listen to
Bach today may find it impossible to resonate to his sacred music" and
regard the texts of such music as "at best irrelevant and at worst distract-
ing. . . . [6] Minear himself acknowledges that whereas Bach composed his
St. Matthew's Passion for a Good Friday service of worship in Leipzig's St.
Thomas Church to complement the sermon, today Bach's great composition is most often performed in a concert hall whose occupants are apt to
be impressed and captivated by the music rather than by the religious message. "The secularization of the *Passion*, therefore . . . marks the reversal
rather than the consummation of Bach's conscious intentions."[7]

This story of Bach's fate as a theologian suggests a paraphrase of the
paradoxical saying of Jesus preserved in the Gospels: whoever would save
the literal meaning of the gospel will lose it, and whoever loses the literal
meaning of the gospel may save it.[8] The case of Bach as theologian shows
that preserving the gospel in its received form does not preserve its meaning in the modern world. In spite of the best of intentions Bach's attempt
to do so failed, and it does not require extraordinary prophetic powers to
predict that the effort of the theological faculty at St. Petersburg and that
of others of similar sincere intention will ultimately fail also. The fact is
that the question of the meaning of the gospel in the modern world is a
fated one: the world changed radically after the seventeenth century and
neither ignoring nor denying the change can resolve the questions of religious meaning the change has raised.

Gain and Loss: The Case of Paul the Convert

The question of gain and loss with respect to religious understanding
and commitment did not arise for the first time in Christian history in the
eighteenth century, of course. One might say that Jesus himself faced it
right at the very beginning of this tradition. One will lose new wine if one
insists upon using old wineskins. One can gain the whole world and lose
one's soul. One can lose one's life by trying to preserve it. The risks are
real, and so are the loss and gain. In taking a risk on the reign of God,
Jesus lost his life, but ultimately gained it, his followers believed.

The most dramatic case that involved a fateful choice between gain
and loss in the generation following Jesus' death was undoubtedly that of
Paul, the converted Pharisee.[9] Some in that first Christian generation
insisted that the new Christian community must not separate itself from

its origins in Judaism. Circumcision, kosher purity and separatism, the authority of scripture and the Mosaic covenant, and the singular sanctity of the temple in Jerusalem must all be retained, they said. To abandon them would be to lose one's hope of salvation. Paul disagreed. He might have tried to be accommodating by consenting to continue the practice of circumcision for its symbolic value, even though he no longer thought it had anything to do with one's salvation; but he didn't. Instead, he argued that circumcision had become irrelevant. His critics accused him of dishonoring the traditions of his fathers and falsifying the gospel. He told them that they were missing the point. Things that once meant everything to him and to them, he said, had become worthless in light of what had been revealed about God's power and grace through the life and death of Jesus. To cling to ethnic credentials when God was offering a new and universal humanity was to cling to what had been trashed by a new reality. It was a colossal failure to grasp the gain of the new situation.[10]

If Paul and other like-minded early Christians had submitted to the demands of their tradition–bound critics, it seems likely that Jesus' gospel would have spawned only a short-lived Jewish sect or have been folded into any of several forms of ancient Gnosticism for a while, and that the gentile church as we know it would never have come into being. What actually happened in history owes much to Paul's ability to recognize gain and loss for what they were and to act on his insights rather than to cling to what he had come to see as a circumscribed and dysfunctional religious tradition.

Gain and Loss: The Case of Galileo and Darwin

The gain and loss issue that impinges upon us most consequentially is undoubtedly that which burst upon the Western world via the discoveries of Galileo and Darwin. Probably no other discoveries have had greater impact on the way we have understood life on earth, on the one hand, and the claims of our religious tradition, on the other. Intellectual historian Richard Tarnas suggests that "as an event that took place not only in astronomy and the sciences but in philosophy and religion and in the collective psyche the Copernican revolution [introduced by Copernicus, confirmed by Kepler and Galileo] can be seen as constituting *the* epochal shift of the modern age. It was a primordial event, world-destroying and world-constituting."[11] Yet four centuries after Galileo and a century and a half after Darwin, much of the Christian world is still mired in dispute about what has been gained and what has been lost for religious faith and life in consequence of these historic breakthroughs in our knowledge about the relation of the earth and the heavens and about human origins and the human person. Modern historical consciousness arose in the wake of Galileo's worldview-altering discoveries and, after Darwin, acquired new perspectives on what it means to be human. Biblical notions of time, space, and the natural world have become ancient ruins, and our view of the human condition and prospect has been radically altered in light of this new knowledge.

Bad as the church's initial response to Galileo's discoveries was, one can understand how difficult it was at the time to respond to an alleged discovery of such shattering significance. Galileo's views were contested by other learned university scholars at the time. He might be proven wrong. The telescope was a recent invention. Perhaps what it brought into view was a distorted image of the heavens. It's no wonder that philosophical as well as religious minds were boggled for a time.

We, on the other hand, have no such excuse. Galileo's recognition of the heliocentric character of our niche in the universe is no longer in dispute. The flat earth society is a joke, not a serious claimant to astronomical knowledge. Although religiously motivated "creationists" pretend to represent a scientifically admissible view of the origins of the cosmos, not even they think that the creation stories of Genesis, as told by their ancient Hebrew authors, are superior to the tale told by the advance of science. It is therefore even more reprehensible and backward for contemporary religionists to cling to circumscribed, outmoded, and dysfunctional beliefs and practices than it was for Galileo's stunned and disoriented contemporaries. Most of them were too traumatized by the prospect of immediate loss to contemplate what might be gained from Galileo's sudden illumination of the way things really are. We, on the other hand, have had ample opportunity to assess the gain this disclosure offers. For at least two centuries now it has been recognized that our challenge in the modern era is to find the wisdom and courage to embrace this knowledge for its undeniable gain, even if it means that some venerable forms of faith are unavoidably lost.[12]

The Jesus Seminar and the Jesus of History

The work of the Jesus Seminar is one prominent current attempt to respond honestly and publicly to this challenge. The Seminar's collaborative effort to find the evidence of the authentic words and deeds of Jesus is an attempt to discover the truth about the Jesus of history by using the investigative methods that have proven to be indispensable in the post-Galileo world—the world we actually live in. The results of our inquiry (and that of other scholars willing to go wherever good historical evidence and sound historical interpretation may lead them) provide the people of the Christian churches and any other interested persons with important resources for constructing an understanding of Christian faith that, in the words of theologian Gordon Kaufman, can help "to sustain and support, to orient and guide, to motivate and refresh ongoing human life."[13] The Seminar's search for the best evidence about the historical Jesus has resulted in the emergence of a figure whose profile and significance can only be seen in terms that are radically different from the figure who is represented in the confessional language of the ancient Christian creeds. One might say, in paradoxical paraphrase of the Apostle Paul, that "although we once regarded Jesus from the ancient creedal point of view, we regard him thus no longer."[14]

In the present situation the churches are faced with both loss and gain. On the one hand, the Jesus of the Nicene Creed and the literal understanding of the meaning of Christian faith bound up with that figure have become an archaeological ruin. We may well find these ancient structures interesting to explore as evidence about religious life in the distant past; but we cannot live in them today. On the other hand, the Jesus of history and his vision of the reign of God in human affairs have been recovered. This is the Jesus whose life and teaching might still be instructive in some ways for living wisely and humanely in our day. The rediscovery of the historical Jesus has shown the Jesus of the Nicene Creed to be a theological fiction that however prominent a role it has played in the Christian past has no credibility or use in the modern world. It is obvious to any thinking observer today that the Nicene Creed locates its Jesus in an eternity that never was and credits him with a divinity he never claimed and never had. The Jesus elevated to the heights of heaven in the eyes of the bishops who gathered at Nicea in the early fourth century CE is literally beyond belief and therefore religiously worthless in the eyes of religiously literate people in the twenty-first century. What remains interesting and credible to us is not the Jesus who is "begotten of God the Father before the creation of the world, God of God, Light of Light, very God of very God . . . being of one substance with the Father," but a young man from the village of Nazareth who envisioned a way to live that challenged tradition and custom, privilege and power, to which vision he committed himself and for which he risked everything. This is not a fairy tale. This is as real as history, and as real as the question of what we should live for and by what criteria we should judge the legitimacy and humanity of our society. It must be acknowledged that as a venture in history, Jesus lost; but as a venture of faith he won. Many have found his way of envisioning life to be liberating and uplifting across the generations.

The Need for Plain Speaking

It is of great importance that we now speak about this clearly, openly, and with conviction. It will not do to try to have it both ways: to insist that it is all right for us to continue to use traditional theological language, since we don't mean it literally anymore. The language of the Nicene Creed was not meant to be understood only symbolically or poetically by those who drafted it in 325 CE nor by most of those who have recited it across the centuries. They understood that what the Creed said about the world was really true and what it said about Jesus was actually so. They did not regard the Creed as just an aesthetically appealing use of religious rhetoric that resonated with a fitting sense of Christian "spirituality." To mouth ancient words of faith while mentally stripping them of their ancient meaning not only has the appearance of duplicity, it also turns them into mumbo-jumbo.

A misguided attempt to affirm a connection between ancient Christian tradition and modern religious understanding by using old religious labels for what were in fact new religious ideas has been going on among some religious modernists for more than a century now. It is not as if this fascile maneuver has not had its critics. In a sermon delivered in 1910, Harvard Divinity School's Dean, William Wallace Fenn, criticized his liberal clergy colleagues for "calling new notions in religion by the old names." The first duty of the theologian, Fenn said, is "to fit his thought to the fact and his word to the thought." The second is "to distinguish between things that differ;" that is, not to pretend that old and new religious ideas do not differ.[15] Again in 1913, Fenn admonished liberals to "stop trying 'to adapt old phrases and usages to fit the religious life of today.' The urgent need of the moment was, instead, 'to aid that religious life in creating its own forms of expression.' "[16] Unfortunately, Fenn wrote, most liberal Protestant clergy in that day were not willing to do this.

> Indeed, readers of current theological literature must often wish that every writer were obliged to furnish a glossary in order that his teaching might be fully intelligible. . . . Until theology writers are willing to cast aside their patched and baggy terminology—the race set before us is not a sack race—they can hardly expect a sympathetic hearing from thoughtful men [sic]. And in addition, looseness and vagueness of utterance inevitably react upon thought. A smear of words and a smouch [smudge] of ideas are reciprocally related. The supreme need of Modern Liberalism, so far as wide appreciation goes, is for definite, precise thinking and direct, plain speaking.[17]

Kingdom of God: The Problem
and Potential of a Religious Symbol

Our situation today requires a reorientation in our religious thinking and speaking, not a papering over of the difference between Nicene orthodoxy and modern religious understanding—and not taking refuge in the halfway house of translating yesterday's literal confessional statements into today's poetic equivocations. To shift from the Jesus of Nicea to the Jesus of history requires us to speak differently about the meaning of the gospel. That the one necessarily follows from the other is immediately apparent to those whose beliefs about Jesus continue to orbit around the Nicene affirmations. "If Jesus did not really come into the world to die on the cross to save us from our sins," a Southern Baptist seminary professor once asked me, "what's the good news?" The good news, I responded, is what Jesus said it was: it is good news about the Kingdom of God. As the naming of the central idea or symbol in Jesus' teaching and of his vision of the good life, that answer is appropriate. The Kingdom of God is indeed what Jesus' teaching is about and is also the goal he was aiming for. But correctly identifying the idea or symbol that was of central importance for the Jesus of history does not furnish us with a theological concept or symbol that can simply be hand-carried directly from the ancient to the modern world intact. For one thing, the Kingdom of God is a political symbol based upon the institution of the monarchy in antiquity. Those in ancient Israel for whom the romantic images of the reigns of David and Solomon furnished an idealistic image of the good society, the idea of God as the ultimate Lord and Ruler of the whole world, both natural and human, was understandable and effective imagery. It captured the essence of Israel's religious ideal. It worked well as a critique of the rule of Rome in the time of Jesus also. But this imagery is inherently authoritarian and carries the problematic of authoritarianism with it: it conveys the notion of finality and demands total submission. The idea of theocracy, the rule of God, is capable of bearing oppressive fruits, as the Taliban have recently demonstrated. These traits are at odds with the nature of a modern democratic society whose citizens regard the idea of monarchy with its centralization of power in a single person as inherently flawed and predisposed toward injustice. A democratic people have come to believe that "power corrupts and absolute power corrupts absolutely," as Lord Acton famously put it. Absolutism is a threat to democratic ideas about freedom and equality. In our religious situation, consequently, there is at least a considerable tension if not a conflict between the notions of kingly rule and individual liberty that did not exist in early Israel nor during the Hellenistic and Roman eras. Ancient imagery and rhetoric often ring differently in modern democratic culture than they did in the period of their origins, and that can sometimes mean not only difference but also dissonance.

There is another compelling reason why it is a mistake to suppose that the task of Christian faith and life today is simply to accept Jesus' teaching about the Kingdom of God and apply it directly to personal, social, and political life in our time: Jesus' vision of the Kingdom of God is a perfectionistic and utopian vision that cannot be fully realized in human life in history. The ancient church recognized this when it embraced the idea of the *parousia*—the coming, later the second coming—of Jesus as Lord at the end of history. That is when the limitations and sinfulness of life in history would be overcome by a miraculous exercise of divine power that would create a new heavens and a new earth in which life would be transformed and made perfect. Then and only then could God's will be done on earth as it is done in heaven. Too often the modern church, perhaps embarrassed by literalistic expectations of the end of the world with its pathetic, spooky fears of being "left behind"[18] and its simpleminded fantasies about life in the world to come, has forgotten the serious point being made in the notion of the *parousia*: that Jesus' vision of life in the Kingdom of God transcends what is possible in history. It is a utopian vision and must be acknowledged as such. Failure to acknowledge that realistic assessment will lead one either to embark on quixotic missions that will lead to failure and disillusionment, or to reject Jesus' vision entirely as a useless fantasy. Fortunately the utopian character of Jesus' vision of life in the Kingdom of God has been noticed by some Christian thinkers, chief among whom in the twentieth century was Reinhold Niebuhr. The pity is that so few seem to have paid him much heed, his considerable visibility and acclaim notwithstanding. The ethic of Jesus transcends what is possible in history, Niebuhr frankly admitted. A life so pure that it *never* pursues its own self-interest (1 Cor 13:5) may do very well among the angels in heaven, but cannot survive in this world. What is true about the relation of Jesus' ethical teaching to the life of the individual is true also of its relation to society. "The ethic of Jesus may offer valuable insights and sources of criticism for a prudential social ethic which deals with present realities," Niebuhr says, "but no such social ethic can be *directly* derived from a pure religious ethic."[19] In the space between the teaching of Jesus and a viable modern social ethic must come our own informed reflection and judgment. Only by such an *indirect* route can the ethic of Jesus bear any useful ethical fruit in modern society.

The folly of confusing visions of righteousness with historical realities and probabilities was pointed out by Niebuhr half a century ago in a little-noticed passage in his book, *Faith and History*. The great eighth century BCE prophet Isaiah predicted that Jerusalem would remain inviolable if Israel put its whole trust in God, but that if it negotiated a defense treaty with Egypt, Jerusalem would be destroyed (Isaiah 31). Events at the time seemed to confirm Isaiah's confidence that history is ruled by the greater righteousness; but in the great prophet Jeremiah's time a century later, Isaiah's faith that righteousness would guarantee security proved to be a snare and a utopian delusion.[20] In Jeremiah's time the Babylonians proved that superior righteousness in Jerusalem did not make that city inviolable (as did the Romans also in 70 CE). Niebuhr observed that

> Isaiah's error reoccurs perennially in the history of Christian thought and life. It consists in the belief that God's providence establishes a special immunity from disaster to a nation which makes itself worthy of such immunity by perfect righteousness. Actually the historical process is not so simply moral. Nations, as well as individuals, may be destroyed not only by violating the laws of life, but also by achieving a defenceless purity, incompatible with the necessities of survival. Ultimately New Testament faith was to revere a Christ whose perfect goodness was validated by an obvious defeat in history. But there are Christian perfectionists who still do not understand *the logic of the Cross*. They hope that if goodness is only perfect enough its triumph in history will be assured.[21]

When we appeal to the teachings of Jesus as a basis for the social ethic we are persuaded to advocate, we should take fully into account "the logic of the cross"—that a goodness so pure that it cannot or will not defend itself will almost always be defeated in this world. Failure to heed this logic will deliver our visions of constructive virtue into the unforgiving hands of destructive folly. Goodness must guide society, if the life of its members has any hope of being worth living, but goodness has never ruled alone in any human society. A just society is possible only if at least some of its members know how to use power to defend and advance the good. "A man [sic] or nation which disavows the use of power as morally too ambiguous to be a means to a good end," Niebuhr remarked, "or which refuses to press its own claims in the competitive claims and counter-claims of life, is not certain of survival. It is, in fact, almost certain to be worsted in the pressures of life."[22] It is up to us now, and not up to Jesus or to the authors of the New Testament, to see to it that this great religious symbol, the Kingdom of God, is not put to thoughtless and fatuous use that undermines its real value as a means of helping us find ways to bring human life in the modern world, as much as is realistically possible, under the rule of the good.

What I have said here so far is aimed at underscoring the necessity of a critical understanding of the good news that the Jesus of history proclaimed and to point to the inadequacy and problematic character of sincere but simpleminded attempts to "put the teachings of Jesus into practice." But if the Kingdom of God as a central religious symbol in Jesus' teaching includes some elements that are problematic for religiously literate moderns, it also retains considerable potential for focusing religious meaning and as a criterion for personal and social ethics. If we recognize that the principal meaning of the Kingdom of God as a religious symbol is its vision of an order of life in which there is a perfect union of power and goodness and that includes all humanity and all creation within its realm of concern and care—i.e., if that is what the symbol of the Kingdom of God is really about—then that symbol can furnish a fruitful basis and motivation for theological reflection and for fostering moral sensitivity and moral responsibility in the modern world. It will be necessary for us to do our own thinking about the meaning and relevance of such an idealistic symbol for modern culture, however, and not simply rely upon quoting scripture.[23]

As the foregoing observations suggest, the idea that we can adequately address the moral and religious needs of our time by simply repeating the answers in the form in which they were given in ancient traditions is mistaken. Relying uncritically upon traditional answers and affirmations fails to take into account the fact that such traditions are the human constructions of an earlier time and are limited by the historical circumstance and understanding of their time of origin (and of the periods during which they were able to transmit their original intention). We can often learn much from noting how our predecessors developed effective forms for affirming their faith; but in the end we must accept responsibility for understanding the meaning of our faith and for developing forms that can effectively and honestly commend such a faith in our own time.[24]

The Principal Challenge Confronting the Churches

Thus far in this essay I have suggested that our religious situation is one in which, like that of the Pharisee Paul after Jesus and like that of the church generally after Galileo, we are inescapably confronted with the prospect of gaining or losing everything; and that the work of the Jesus Seminar is one prominent attempt to respond to the challenge of that situation. The Seminar's work has had the effect of obliging us to come to terms with an unavoidable loss: the iconic, authoritarian Jesus of Nicea has become impotent and irrelevant. That icon has fallen from its high altar and broken into pieces, like the item of sacred statuary it was, with the collapse of the ancient and medieval worldview that Galileo's telescope had exposed as no longer credible. The Seminar's work has also enabled us to recover a profile of the Jesus of history and to sketch both the problem and the potential of the idea of the Kingdom of God that was at the center of his life and teaching. It remains in this brief essay to name the principal task confronting the churches in light of these developments. In a word, that challenge is *education*.

The rueful fact is that the only version of Christian faith that most people both inside and outside of the churches are conversant with is that of the Nicene orthodoxy that has come undone with the advent of the modern world. A good number of people have their doubts about and their discomfort with the archaic claims of traditional Christianity, to be sure, but few of them have the means for constructing a new form of Christian faith that is congruent with and capable of enlightening their experience in the modern world. When asked to say what they believe, many otherwise-articulate people become virtually mute, or fall back on platitudes or wander off into vague talk about "spirituality." It's no wonder. We can no more expect people to embrace a new understanding of Christian faith in the absence of information that shows why it is necessary and what its contours are than we could expect people to give up their visually reinforced notion that the sun arcs around the earth in the absence of convincing information about the solar system. Only a few need to become astronomers, but everyone needs a readable map of our corner of the universe. A viable faith also requires a readable map. An adequate faith is not possible in the absence of the requisite knowledge.

A recent editorial in *The Christian Century* reported that a German church consultant, after collecting data from one thousand congregations in thirty-two countries, has concluded that "all growing congregations have eight traits in common: leaders who empower others to do ministry; ministry tasks distributed according to the gifts of members; a passionate spirituality marked by prayer and putting faith into practice; organizational structures that promote ministry; inspiring worship services; small groups in which the loving and healing power of fellowship is experienced; need-oriented evangelism that meets the needs of people the church is trying to reach; and loving relationships among the members of the church."[25] Noticeably missing from this list is any mention of teaching and learning, any reference to biblical or theological literacy, or any reference of any kind to what people have come to *know* and *understand* about their faith.

Apparently churches today can flourish even though their members do not know or believe anything important enough to be perceived as a significant factor in their growth as organizations or in the lives of their members. Apparently "inspirational" gatherings, social service, and being a nice group of people to be a part of "meets the needs" both of the people already in such churches as well as those whom they are trying to reach. Despite this glowing report about today's dynamic churches, one wonders how long communities of faith can continue in the absence of any serious attention to what is referred to by the word "faith." Does a tree produce foliage and bear fruit after its roots wither? That would really be a miracle. Someone once said that "piety may be the religion of the moment, but theology is the religion of the generations." Traits of growth at the moment notwithstanding, it is highly probable that what the people of the church do or do not *know* and *believe* will ultimately prove to be fateful for the generations.

In an unrelated column in the same issue of the *Century* the author remarks on a noticeable change in the language commonly used to speak about the religious dimension of our lives. "We have moved away from 'faith' to 'spirituality,' " he says. "The talk of 'faith' rightly emphasizes cognitive and moral content and life in community; the talk of 'spirituality,' on the other hand, is cognitively and morally vague and emphasizes the empowerment and healing of autonomous individuals." In part, the author suggests, this shift in language reflects the fact that in a marketplace culture, religion "is in danger of degenerating into yet another consumer good:" something to be used when needed and to be discarded or placed in storage when not. In contrast to these recent developments, he says, "every great theology [in the history of Christian faith] has been a vision of a way of life."[26] It is a poor bargain to exchange a vision of a way of life for religious consumer goods, even if the latter bring a crowd to the store. In the meantime the faith by which such consumers of religion really live is drawn not from their religious life but from secular sources: political and economic beliefs; the glitter culture of celebrity; the easy sensual beat of popular culture; secular gospels promising personal health, wealth, and success.

An earlier age valued the idea of a learned clergy. Harvard College was founded in 1636 to ensure that the growing colonial population in New England would be served by a clergy that was up to the job. There is no going back to the time when theology was generally regarded as "the queen of the sciences" and when the Protestant minister was often the best-educated man in town—and there is no need to indulge in such nostalgia. What does need recognition is that there is even more need for a learned clergy and for religiously knowledgeable congregations now than there was then. In a time when education has come to play an indispensable role in virtually all of our life experience, it has become indispensable in our religious lives as well. In that earlier era an educated clergy was needed to enhance the authority of the church and its faith. In the present era an educated clergy and a religiously knowledgeable people are needed to deal with the question of the credibility and relevance of the church and its faith.

Designing a New Style of Worship

How can the education of the people of the church that our religious situation calls for be accomplished? An important part of an answer to that question is already under way in some churches: adult education series and programs, special classes, and small groups in which recently published biblical and theological scholarship that is addressed to a general audience is read and discussed. The Jesus Seminar on the Road programs have been well-received sources of stimulation and education for an ever-increasing number of churches. All of these means can continue to be utilized to advantage. But there is another avenue that is at least as important as any of these and in some respects is even more important: the form and content of public worship. Too often the kinds of educational programs just mentioned go on with no visible effect upon the conduct of public worship. They remain marginal activities, more often tolerated than utilized. This pattern continues the virtual divorce between biblical scholarship and the church's worship that has prevailed, for the most part, throughout the modern era. What if scholarship and worship remarried? What would Christian public worship look like:

- If the Jesus honored in it were the historical Jesus of first-century Palestine rather than the iconic Jesus of fourth-century Nicea?
- If the Kingdom of God as a symbol of the claims of the order of nature and of the moral ideal on our life as humans became the central paradigm of worship rather than the notions of sin and forgiveness derived from a theory about the cross as the sacrifice God required as payment for human offenses against the divine honor and righteousness?
- If in our worship we aimed to reflect the evolutionary-historical and sociohistorical conceptions of the human person and the astrophysical and ecological conceptions of the earth and the universe that, Galileo-like, have been made visible to us in the course of the development of modern knowledge—rather than to continue to make

the Genesis stories of creation our principal point of reference about these matters simply because they are "biblical"? [27]

- If, in short, worship were designed to reflect the reality of the world as we know it and humanity's place in it with the aim of helping us find our way through it?[28] (This is not a new idea. The great cathedral at Reims, France, with its elaborately sculptured and originally painted Western façade was intended to be a link connecting earth and heaven, our guide told us, portraying the reality and order of the whole world to the understanding of all worshipers and enabling them to see the relation of their own lives to it.)

How might one set out to design such a form of worship? If one were to set out from the work of the Jesus Seminar, a pertinent place to begin would be with the way in which scripture is presented. Common liturgical formulas bracket scripture readings by references to them as "the Word of God," thus affirming their authority as in some way divine in origin. Usually such reading of scripture is offered with little or no comment about its time and place of origin or the connection of the passage selected to the writing as a whole of which it is a part. In a new form of worship as I am envisioning it here, scripture would be presented as our primary source of information about the origins and early history of the faith of the church. In other words, the biblical writings should be presented as the church's earliest classical literature. As such these scriptures are the word of humans about God and about human life viewed as under God's sovereignty, not the word of God. That is, God (and God's alleged rule) is the *subject* of these scriptures, not their *author*. The biblical authors were concerned with throwing light upon human history and experience in the hope of leading it to a good end. As the word of our religious progenitors about God, the biblical scriptures are an irreplaceable source of information about the origins of a characteristic way of viewing the human situation and a primary resource for theological reflection. Such a view of scripture is consistent with the way critical biblical scholars look at the Bible and with the methods they use to recover historical information embedded in these writings as well as the faith or religious meaning their authors affirm. To make effective use of this scholarship for the purposes of worship, I suggest, every passage of scripture read in public worship should be accompanied by information about its author, the time and place of its composition, the situation the author addressed, and the point the author wanted to make. It is the view of human life expressed in the text that needs to be made evident, or the issue raised by the text for our consideration, criticism, reflection, and on occasion for updating and correction. This way of using scripture in worship is to treat it as a valuable resource for our reflection and enlightenment, but not as an anthology of divine pronouncements nor as a compendium of eternal truths that must not be questioned.

The necessary information about the scripture read in worship can be variously conveyed: by a well-prepared introduction to the reading delivered orally, or printed as an insert in the church bulletin or order of worship, or incorporated into the sermon. But without this information scripture reading will be left either to the vagaries of free-association by the hearer, to the superstitious notion that biblical words are endowed with supernatural power and inexhaustible meanings, or to dismissal as incomprehensible or irredeemably antiquated and irrelevant. The reading of scripture in public worship is a prime teachable moment in which the marriage of faith and scholarship should be visibly and audibly celebrated. Such a practice would do much to provide worshipers with some of the most important information they need to move toward a form of Christian faith that is both modern in its literacy and credible in its claims. *Information is the source of inspiration about the contemporary meaning of Christian faith.*

This proposal does not assume that the sanctuary is to be regarded simply as a classroom, but it does assume that it is *essential* for worshipers to know what they are reading or hearing when scripture is included as an element of worship. Remember, we are admonished by "the great commandment" to love God with all our mind, as well as with our heart, soul, and strength. The commandment assumes that these four are and ought to be inseparable. May it be so![29]

If the Jesus of history and his vision of the Kingdom of God as the symbol of the union of power and goodness that ought to rule in human life constitutes the central paradigm for a new form of Christian worship, and if a new way of presenting and understanding the value and importance of scripture became a regular part of that worship, other appropriate changes would follow, some of which I can mention here, but only briefly.

One such change would be in the language we use about Jesus. If Jesus is not the divine being elevated to complete equality with God the Father at Nicea, and if earlier intimations of divinity such as that in the story of his being born of a virgin are seen as affirmations of faith, not "ontological facts," then references to Jesus as Lord, Savior, Redeemer become religiously dysfunctional for moderns. These titles are all dependent upon the credibility of the ancient biblical worldview, according to which God rules over nature and history from the divine throne high in the heavens. The literal statements about Jesus being Lord, Savior, Redeemer have lost their literal meaning with the advent of the modern understanding of the world.[30] From the perspective of a modern historical consciousness, Jesus is the pioneer and exemplar of Christian faith: he is the visionary teacher and leader who looked at life as if it were under the rule of divine goodness (which is, of course, a union of power and goodness, the rule of God being a rule of power and not a rule of goodness only) and who had the courage and integrity to commit himself unconditionally to that ideal. A modern democratic people can understand and even venerate a man of such vision, courage, and integrity; but not many religiously literate moderns will find it either possible or meaningful to think of Jesus as our divine Lord, whether on earth or "in heaven." Gaining the Jesus of history and his religious vision inevitably involves losing Jesus the divine being.

Traditional references to Jesus as Savior and Redeemer also reflect the ancient biblical worldview and are specifically based upon the theory that Jesus' crucifixion is to be understood as a sacrificial offering that paid the price for our sins. This notion is in fact an inference drawn by some of Jesus' followers who were trying to make sense of his life and fate by using the means of religious interpretation available to them at the time; but Jesus never made such claims about himself, nor need religiously literate moderns be bound by the theological inferences drawn by his premodern followers. Moderns must have their own reasons for thinking that Jesus is religiously significant. *what are my reasons?*

3. The hymnody of the church presents a major challenge to anyone who would like to modernize public worship. Some of the great traditional hymns may still be able to give expression to the meaning of Christian faith in a modern form of worship, but the lyrics of many hymns voice forms of Christian faith that reflect Nicene orthodoxy and the various forms of piety that have grown out if it. Some of these hymns may survive by giving them substantially new lyrics. Others will no doubt have to be abandoned as the relics of an earlier age. (Recall the case of Bach.) In any case, dealing with the heritage of Christian hymnody is a large project and will be accomplished only through the creativity and the religiously literate imagination of many gifted people.

4. One other change that a new form of worship calls for that can be mentioned briefly here is the form and content of public prayer. As has often been noted, the style of much traditional prayer is that of a lowly subject in the presence of royalty. The pray-er assumes the role of a supplicant who with great deference requests the favor of the divine majesty. That posture presumably seemed fitting in the culture of the ancient and medieval worlds, but seems remote from the world of the modern West. Furthermore, the weekly use of the prayer of confession and assurance of

Does it request favor of a deity?

forgiveness that is still a part of traditional worship in many Protestant churches owes more to ancient orthodoxy's theological paradigm of sin and forgiveness and to liturgical habits corresponding to it than to the actual lives of the people who assemble for worship. The weekly ritual of confessions of sin by a Christian congregation appears to assume that the people of the church are capable of nothing in the future other than repeating the same pathetic failures every week their whole lives long. The real life experience of most worshipers, I submit, is quite different. They are most often people who recognize that they are part of a larger order of life for which they feel gratitude and have a measure of responsibility. They are more likely to be looking for encouragement and wisdom than they are for forgiveness. We should reserve the matters of confession and forgiveness for occasions when something really important has gone wrong that calls for a change of mind and behavior, and abandon the weekly routine of asking forgiveness for doing what we ought not to have done and for leaving undone what we ought to have done. Most of the people for whom such a traditional prayer is relevant are candidates for an appearance in a criminal court or are in prison, not in church.

Conclusion: A Matter of Life and Death

This essay is an invited response to the question posed by Robert Funk as the theme of the Spring 2003 Meeting of Westar Institute: how is the Jesus Seminar related to the faith and life of the church? I do not regard my response merely as an academic exercise nor as a promotional piece on behalf of the Seminar. It is, rather, an attempt to get at the basic truth and meaning of the Christian tradition, from one angle of vision, and to seek what may best preserve its value in a new period of history in which we have come to see our world and ourselves in ways our ancient and medieval predecessors could not have imagined. Some readers may regard the essay as excessively immodest, particularly if they are hoping to gain the advantages of modern knowledge without losing anything from the luggage of the Christian tradition. Trying to have it both ways may look like the soul of caution, but usually proves to be a good way to lose everything without gaining much of anything. The essay accepts the risks of a higher hope.

I find that my own sense of our religious situation and what it requires of us is similar in some important respects to that of theologian Gordon Kaufman. Our attempt to respond to such requirements, he suggests,

> will not be widely effective . . . if it is largely backward-looking and nostalgic, attempting to keep alive outmoded and

irrelevant patterns of praxis and symbolization simply because
they are believed to express "the faith . . . once delivered to the
saints" (Jude 3). . . . Our inherited symbolism no longer fits the
overall cast of life as it is lived, understood, and experienced in
today's world. So it must change, and change in decisive ways, if
it is to continue to function properly—that is, if it is not to die
out.

    Change in matters as deeply important to human life as reli-
gious symbolism is often difficult and painful; yet it happens all
the time, as the history of every religion makes clear. The proper
question to put with respect to Christian patterns of religious
meaning, then, is not, Will (or should) change occur in the present modes of symbolization and praxis of the churches? But
rather, Are the churches willing and able to support the kind of
moves that will enable Christian rituals and symbolism to
continue their life-giving functions? . . . This can happen only, I
think, if there is fairly wide recognition that this is really a life-
or-death-matter for the churches; and that they are, therefore,
required by their own deepest commitments . . . to adapt their
practices and to reconstruct and reconceive the symbols which
they cherish.[31]

Kaufman's characterization of the task before us as a life-or-death matter may seem to some grossly exaggerated. I doubt that it would seem so to
the Apostle Paul. He recognized what was at stake when he saw himself
confronted with the prospect of gaining and losing everything.

Read : "WHY THE CHURCH MUST
CHANGE OR DIE" - SPONG

If You Give a Mouse a Cookie...
What the Quest Holds in Store for the Church

Stephen J. Patterson

If You Give a Mouse a Cookie . . .

With small children at home, most of my metaphors seem to come from the world of children's literature, where many gems wait to be discovered by the unsuspecting adult, gems as profound as they are simple. *If You Give a Mouse a Cookie*[1] is a little tale of tumbling, tangled, domino effects—the unfolding, surprising consequences of taking the first step. "If you give a mouse a cookie, he's going to ask for a glass of milk," and a straw, and a napkin to wipe his milk mustache, and a pair of nail scissors to trim his hair, and a broom, and a nap, and a story. . . . And so you are off on a series of misadventures you never would have dreamed possible when you first opened the cookie jar. In connection with our work in the Jesus Seminar, we have all had opportunities to share our results with church communities, sometimes in the form of a Jesus Seminar on the Road, and more often in local churches closer to home. What happens in a church when the material we are developing is introduced there? When we open the cookie jar of biblical scholarship and the quest for the historical Jesus, what are the consequences that begin to tumble out? What questions are raised? What challenges are encountered? And do people and their communities of faith change?

A few years ago one of our Doctor of Ministry students, Michael Castle, decided to explore these questions in a thesis project centered on his own Midwestern, suburban church.[2] He wanted to see how his parishioners would respond when exposed to the work of critical scholarship.

Would it be the deathblow to Christian faith, as many have argued of late, or could it be the source of new life and energy in his congregation? Castle used the work of several members of the Jesus Seminar, around which he formed weekly study groups. The course of study was to focus on the historical Jesus. What Castle found—and what I suspect many have also experienced—was that the discussion was hard to keep on track. When you raise the historical Jesus question, it seems, other questions are soon to follow. "If you give a mouse a cookie. . . . "

The First Question: <u>What is the Bible?</u>

The minute one begins to speak of the historical Jesus, that is, Jesus as historians might reconstruct him, not as he is presented in the gospels, a question arises for most Christians that is far more important than "What did Jesus say?" or "What did Jesus do?" These questions pale in comparison to the real question on everyone's mind: Is the Bible trustworthy? This question arises quite naturally. If Jesus was not just as he is described in the Bible, then can we rely on the Bible in the way we have been taught by our tradition? This is the first question that arises in most church settings, from the most conservative to the most liberal. A large number of Christians in mainline Protestant and Catholic churches still persist in a kind of unexamined biblical literalism, assuming that the Bible is a historically accurate document and the gospels offer us a kind of collective biography of Jesus.[3] The question of the Bible's trustworthiness arose immediately in Dr. Castle's congregation, a new church founded as an Open and Affirming[4] church in the United Church of Christ. Even among these ultra-liberals this sort of unexamined biblical literalism was the operative view for many of those who participated in his study.[5] Any discussion of the historical Jesus will inevitably have to deal with this question, and usually as a first step. My own experience in churches suggests that the Bible is much more precious to most believers than Jesus (outranked, perhaps, only by cherished hymnals). Seldom has anyone been ruffled by something I might have said about Jesus himself. But challenge the reliability of the Bible, and the house just might come down.

Though widespread among Christians, the literalist view of the Bible is not very secure among mainline Protestants and Catholics (fundamentalists, for whom biblical inerrancy is the first article of faith, are another matter). It is a crystalline vase that will shatter with the slightest tap, if directed to the right place. The most vulnerable spot is perhaps the mythic worldview so obviously presupposed by the Bible, a point recognized and exploited so effectively by Bultmann.[6] Pedagogically, this is a good place to start. Read, for example, Luke's account of the ascension of Jesus in

∴ WE QUESTION - WHO WROTE IT? WHEN, UNDER WHAT CONDITIONS→HISTORICALLY, CULTURALLY, PSYCHOLOGICALLY

Acts 1:6–11. Never mind that this is the second ascension in Luke's account (see Luke 24:51). Focus on the fact that Jesus is carried up into the sky. This, of course, presupposes the three-tiered universe, with heaven above and hell below, that most people on careful consideration will clearly reject as inadequate today. Or read through one of the gospels, calling attention to the large role played by evil spirits and demons. Many of us enjoy horror films, but we do not structure our lives around possible interference from evil spirits stalking our every move. People who do are judged to be so out of touch with reality that they are locked up for their own protection. *HAVE WE MISSED BY SETTLING ON AN ORTHODOX VIEW, THE ESSENTIAL TRUTH?*

This line of questioning, of course, ought not to be an end in itself. As this house of cards comes tumbling down, one must be ready for a series of new questions to be addressed before the discussion can return to the historical Jesus. If the Bible is not literally true, then how is it true, if at all? If scripture is not scientifically or historically reliable, is it reliable in other ways? Is scripture "inspired"? What, finally, *is* scripture, and what is its authority in the life of the Christian? Closely related to this discussion is the question of the biblical canon. This might not arise until the issue of sources for historical Jesus research is broached. But it could arise already here in connection with the question of biblical authority. Why do we venerate the books of the Bible? What distinguishes them from other books? How were these books chosen and not others?

This question of biblical authority is a most vexing issue for liberals today. Most of us think we still want a Bible, but we are hard pressed to say exactly why. Usually we are reduced to mumbling something vague about the value of tradition. Anyone who would introduce the work of the Jesus Seminar into a congregational setting must be prepared to lead folk through these issues with clarity and forthrightness.

My own answers to these questions are no more adequate or profound than the vagaries about which I have just complained. However, there are *3 points* three points that I generally like to make in church settings that seem to be helpful in opening new ways of thinking about scripture. The first may seem obvious, but I find that when speaking with people who have not thought critically about scripture, it cannot be overstated. It is simply that *1.* "history" and "truth" are not the same thing. Whatever we might say about the historicity of this or that saying or tradition, we will not have said anything yet about its value in conveying something true about human existence lived before God. Jesus was a great truth teller. But there are true things that he did not say, that waited to be said by others who followed in his footsteps. And we might even question whether everything Jesus did say was in fact true. For example, Mark presents a memory

Did Jesus say everything attributed to him?
history vs "truth telling"
history ≠ truth

of Jesus calling a Gentile woman a "dog" (Mark 7:27). We need to challenge the modernist assumption that "history" equals "truth."

The second is a point that Helmut Koester has recently argued quite eloquently in an essay entitled, "Writings and the Spirit: Authority and Politics in Ancient Christianity."[7] As surprising as this may seem to modern Christians used to thinking about their Bible as "inspired by the Holy Spirit," the earliest Christians did not think this about their writings. Early Christian communities were certainly what we might call "spirit-filled," replete with manifestations of spiritual ecstasy—prophecy, tongue-speaking, and the like. But this is the point: they located this spiritual activity in the life of their communities, not in the activity of writing. The first to speak of Christian writings as "inspired" by God was, apparently, Clement of Alexandria, who used this idea not to guarantee the historical accuracy of the writings, but to account for the secret meanings he found encoded allegorically beneath the obvious and most surface reading of the text. This interpretive strategy and its theological underpinnings were part of a long Alexandrian school tradition practiced by pagans and Jews long before Clement tried it with Christian texts, but it was not generally how early Christians approached their writings. Our notion that the Bible is inspired by God is a secondary development, not at all to be taken for granted.

The third is that the New Testament canon of scripture was very slow in developing. Our own concept of "the Bible," that is, a single book containing a set of scriptures—always the same set, in the same order, like chapters in a book—is not very old. We must remember that before the invention of the printing press, such a concept of "book" was not really possible. "Bibles" before Gutenburg were made by hand, with scribes assembling texts into various manuscripts, no two of which were exactly alike. Our ancient biblical manuscripts are all unique, the result of scribes preparing collections of their favorite texts, or more likely, those texts most frequently used in their communities. This is what a "bible" was before Gutenburg. It was only when printing made it possible to produce thousands of copies of a book, each exactly the same, that our notion of the book, and our notion of the Bible as *the* Book, become possible. The first councilor decision on the contents of the New Testament was not taken until the Council of Florence in 1442, about the same time the technology of printing was becoming available.[8] The occasion was the incorporation of the Syrian Jacobites, who had not considered James, Revelation, or the catholic epistles scriptural, into the Western church. Ecumenism had brought disparate parts of the church, and their respective canons, together before. Now, for the first time, the sharing of common texts required a formal decision. The first decision on the contents of the Bible as a whole did not come until the Council of Trent in 1546. Trent, of course, was the crowning event of the counter-Reformation, which attempted to throw up key battlements against the new proposals spreading rapidly through the Lutheran lands. Among those reforms of Luther, recall, was the creation of a German vernacular translation of the Bible (1522), in which several texts from Jerome's Bible were not included. In addition to omitting the Old Testament books thought then to be of Greek origin (the Old Testament Apocrypha), Luther also excluded four books from the New Testament: James, Jude, Hebrews, and Revelation. They were not "scripture" to him, for they did not preach Christ. How we come to have a New Testament in the reformed branch of the church today that contains all of these books—or for that matter, why it is that most of the Bibles on my shelves today include Luther's rejected Apocrypha—is a publishing story too long to tell. Suffice it to say, the Bible is not the eternal, unchanging reality our higher views of biblical authority might suggest or require. We need to cultivate lower, more realistic and contingent views of biblical authority more mindful of the Bible's actual history and our actual use of it.

All of this is to suggest that the Bible has whatever value and authority it has for us not because it is directly inspired by God or without error in every respect, but because its texts have, over time, proven to be useful in the cultivation of Christian faith. If the authority of the Bible is in question today, it is not because of doubts about its historical accuracy, but because of doubts that have arisen about particular, biblically supported, Christian ideas and practices that no longer seem valid, such as the assumed inferiority of women, the sinfulness of homosexuality, or the infidelity of "the Jews." One of the great challenges of the church in this generation is to clarify what we actually believe about the Bible and its role in our lives. We need a theory, as Luther had, to guide us in making decisions about what we read in the Bible: When does it speak truth, and when does it not?

The Second Question: Who is God?

Once the tacit assumption that the Bible is historically accurate has been exposed and dealt with, one might assume that one would be freed to proceed with the discussion of the historical Jesus without further interruption. But this is unlikely. For as you return to the gospels and begin to read them critically, now relieved of the assumption of inerrancy, the first thing that will fall under the shadow of post-enlightenment doubt will be the many miraculous stories about Jesus. Some will simply regard the miracles as impossible and wish to go on. But others will want to ask why such things should be impossible. Was not Jesus God's Son? And are not all things possible for God? Why, then, should we doubt the power of Jesus to perform miracles? Your next question has to do with Jesus, God, and power.[9] *PEOPLE ASSUME, EVERYBODY KNOWS*

God is, for most Christians, first and foremost "Almighty God." God's most significant characteristic is *power.* God is omnipotent. This is beyond question. The problem with this belief, of course, is that it conflicts with common experience. Most peoples' experience does not include direct exposure to God's power manifested in miraculous deeds. Moreover, most are skeptical of second-hand reports of the miraculous. When cardiac arrest strikes, we turn to doctors to do their work and hope for the best. The wise pastor offers prayers for support and encouragement, but not for a miracle. If anything miraculous occurs, it is strictly in the eye of the beholder. Of course, there are some for whom "Touched by An Angel" is more than entertaining television. Stories of the miraculous, even angelic T.V. fantasies, are the very substance of Christian faith. To such folk, modern skepticism about such things is a grave manifestation of unfaith. To doubt God's power and God's willingness to intervene in our lives is to doubt the very existence of God. These will be troubled discussions requiring great care.

While most liberal believers will have realized the problem miracles pose to the modern worldview, they may not have realized the depth of the *theological* problem posed by the miracles of Jesus and the almighty God who stands behind them.[10] What shall we make of a God who possesses the power to control human events, but does nothing to prevent millions from starving, does not protect the innocent from abuse, does not rescue victims from natural disaster? If God is omnipotent, but does not use this all-power for good, how can we imagine this God as good at all? Could such a God be anything more than a sadistic voyeur toying with the lives of helpless victims? An omnipotent God could only be a monster God, not at all related to the gracious God known to Jesus and Paul.

This problem of theodicy, or God's relationship to evil and suffering, has plagued Jewish and Christian theologians for centuries. The author of the biblical book of Job grappled with it, unsuccessfully in my view. When God and Satan hatch a plot to test Job's loyalty by subjecting him to unfathomable sufferings, the best retort God can manage to Job's angry lament is: Who are you to question my inscrutable ways? "Have you an arm like God, and can you thunder with a voice like his?" (Job 40:9). Here is the angry father God, who does not like to be questioned by his children. Augustine defended his seemingly cruel and unjust God—the God who would punish even the tiniest baby for the original sin conveyed to all by Adam—with another common answer to this question: "You must distinguish the justice of God from human ideas of justice."[11] This is a clever response, for it rests on the uncontestable assumption that God's ways and those of humans are not to be compared. But if Augustine's God, and the God of Job, is not really God after all, but the product of a flawed human imagination incapable of conceptualizing God as anything other than an angry super-human tyrant, then Augustine's God is skewered on his own petard. In fact, the angry God of Augustine, who pursues "His awesome blood-feud against the family of Adam,"[12] is all too human, and, like the God of Job, not a mystery at all.

Theologians have seen this problem through the centuries. How can God be both good and all-powerful when the universe is filled not just with God's glory, but also with bad people who do bad things? For some, the solution to this dilemma lies in God's graciousness. In God's graciousness, God gives humans the freedom to do as they will. God is still omnipotent, but chooses not to exercise this all-power by intervening in human events. From this grant of freedom springs moral responsibility. But would such a God be truly good? I want my own children to be free to make choices, to learn to exercise moral judgment and just plain common good sense. But would I be a good father if, for the sake of that freedom, I failed to intervene in their fighting or allowed them to wander into traffic? If such a human father would be charged with neglect, why shouldn't God the "father"? In a post-Holocaust world, a God who gives us our freedom is still a very disturbing deity. Others have argued that God has actually given up power, and so could not intervene even if God wished. But this, of course, presumes a power in the universe superior even to God's omnipotence, a super-power capable of enforcing such a bargain. And if this is theologically problematic, and God turns out to be God's own police force preventing God from reclaiming the power once laid down, then this is really no different from God—both policer and policed—simply deciding not to exercise power.

Both of these theories about God's power ultimately turn out to be rear-guard actions designed simply to protect a bad idea: the omnipotence of God. As theologically disastrous as omnipotence turns out to be in relation to purely human activity, consider where the idea leads when one takes in the realm of natural phenomena, disaster, and disease. What if the value of human freedom is not at stake, but merely the flourishing of a virus, the adjustment of tectonic plates, or the violent swirling of winds? Does God have a virtuous, but hidden, purpose for allowing such things to wreak havoc on innocent lives? Or if human failings could somehow account for these minor disasters or their resultant sufferings, what if by chance an asteroid should plow into the earth, as has happened at least once before in the history of the planet, destroying all life as we know it? Could such a God initiating, executing, and controlling the event be described reasonably as "loving," "compassionate," or "just" in relation to human beings? Even the God of judgment does not fit this picture very well, insofar as these things are truly random in their effects. AIDS affects the moral and the immoral alike, the young and the old, the male and the female, the rich and the poor (but especially the poor).

The miracles of Jesus, as an instance of God's power, are directly relevant here, for, taken as history, they assert God's power to intervene precisely in such circumstances. But in exploring the depth of this problem we have seen that it is profound indeed. If Jesus, as God's agent, can intervene in the natural order of things, it is only because God is Lord of the created world. But if the creation reveals anything about the creator, it is that we are not at the center of the creator's universe, that the creator does not ultimately care about our fate, does not love us, does not number the hairs on each human head, and does not even judge us by any known standard of justice. The creation is violent and chaotic. Now, we might return to Augustine and say that one should not equate God's way of caring with our ways, or God's love with our love, or God's justice with our justice. But these are all human terms and concepts—care, love, justice—with approximate meanings derived from the realm of human affairs. If they do not really apply when we talk about God, we should not use them anymore and try instead for the most approximately appropriate words: unpredictable, arbitrary, dangerous.

Of course, all of these blasphemies arise from a single root cause: the mistaken idea of omnipotence. If we give up this idea, they too disappear. If God is not all-powerful, then God is not all-responsible, and so is not defined by all that is. Without the whole universe bearing witness to God's character, we are free to proclaim God as good, if that is indeed how we experience God. Reinhold Niebuhr saw this with characteristic clarity 75 years ago, when in seconding Albert Schweitzer's return to the qualified dualism so typical of much of our scriptural tradition, he wrote: "To make God responsible for the universe is to rob him of his goodness. The facts of life are simply too confused to warrant faith in a God who is at once good and omnipotent."[13] Instead Niebuhr casts his lot with a God who is not all-powerful, but who joins in the battle on the side of good against evil. His God is really much more like the God of Jesus, whose power to heal and exorcise demons is wielded not against God's own handiwork, but against the forces of evil who, in the mythic world of the New Testament, are powers in their own right, arrayed against God and God's agent, Jesus. Even the creator God of Genesis is not really the omnipotent God of classical theism. Rather, this God creates by driving back the chaos and dividing the mysterious waters of the deep, the Ancient Near Eastern mythic depiction of danger and disaster. It is God against evil, not God against God.

Giving up on the omnipotence of God will not be easy. It will mean, first of all, that we must accept that we live in a universe of chance. The existence of God does not change that. Events might happen to us that have no real purpose or meaning. There is no master plan. The future lies open, full of possibilities, both good and evil. All we can say is that if God is good, then God sides with good against evil. But God's power is (obviously) not such that it can guarantee a result. Then what is the nature and extent of God's power? Is love a power? Is justice?

Perhaps the most difficult thing about giving up on omnipotence is the questions this will leave unanswered. For many, even the poor answers offered by the theory of omnipotence will be preferable to the angst created by no answers at all. Of these questions, none is more frightening than the question of existence itself. As we have seen, it is the violence and chaos of the natural realm that poses one of the greatest difficulties for reconciling the goodness of God with omnipotence. What if the goodness of God cannot be reconciled with the idea that God creates and sustains the universe? Then we will have to choose between believing in the goodness of God and the power of God to create. But if God is not the creator of the universe, then why do things exist? Where do we come from? Why are we here? These questions can be paralyzing. Expect a retreat, precisely here.

Third Question: Is Jesus God?

The courageous will go on, though perhaps a little bewildered. Now at least, at last, it might be possible to begin talking about Jesus. With the question of biblical authority behind us, and the question of God's power broached, if not settled, perhaps the way has been cleared.

Not so fast. For many Christians, Jesus is of interest because he is the Son of God. The Bible, which provides an objective historical account of the remarkable events surrounding his life, including the miracles he performed, and especially the greatest miracle of them all, his physical resurrection from the dead, is what tells us that Jesus is indeed the Son of God. But if the Bible is *not* history, and the miracles are not to be believed *as miracles*, then what remains to suggest that we should be interested in Jesus at all? Is he still God's Son? And if this cannot be proven from an inerrant scripture or a miracle-filled history, is he still worthy of studied attention and devotion? What is left?

What is left are the words and deeds of Jesus. At first blanche this may seem like small potatoes compared to miracles, the resurrection, and the inspired Word of God. But in fact it is not. Miracles were not unthinkable in the ancient world. Every religious figure could lay claim to a few. In comparison to others', Jesus' miracles are not particularly astounding. The healing stories surrounding him would have struck most as the activity of a common exorcist. But what of the resurrection? Was that not something special, something unique? No. Resurrection, resuscitation, translation to heaven—these are part of the common stock of Mediterranean religion. Moreover, the resurrection stories of early Christianity are easily falsified. An appearance of Jesus could be taken as nothing more than a ghost story; an empty tomb is a stolen body. These are not the proofs we might take them to be from a distance of 2000 years. As confessions of faith, these early Christian claims are of infinite value, but we must not imagine them as evidence capable of proving the Christian case.

What made Jesus, and the religion of Jesus, unique and compelling was nothing other than the words he spoke and the things he did. For the earliest followers of Jesus his words and deeds were everything. Consider those who first heard Jesus, believed he was right, and decided to follow him. What did they have to go on? Was Jesus so obviously divine that anyone who heard him would have immediately dropped everything to become a devotee? Did he have a halo? Of course not. Did he spice his performances with miracles so that all would know who he really was? Ridiculous. What these early followers of Jesus had to go on were the same things by which any of us must make judgments about those whom we encounter: what a person says and does. And here is the astonishing thing: many of those who heard Jesus and believed him, who experienced him and followed him, followed in such a way that radically disrupted and changed their lives forever. Whether one believes that the Jesus movement was an itinerant movement of social radicals (Theissen), or a village-centered movement of radical transformation (Horsley), apocalyptically inspired (Allison), or centered in prophetic wisdom (Koester), to become part of the Jesus movement was a radical step.

> Go, sell what you own and give to the poor . . . then come and follow me.[14]
> Unless you hate your father and mother, brother and sister, you cannot be my disciple.[15]
> I came not to bring peace, but a sword.[16]

The followers of Jesus embraced these sayings because they embraced Jesus, whose words and deeds moved them. His parables convinced them that the world could be different. His aphorisms sabotaged their view of the world and brought them new clarity of vision. His open table fellowship introduced a way of being in community that was at once threatening and inviting, as honor was extended to the shamed, inclusion to the ostracized. His exorcisms proved nothing except that here was a person with the power to make you clean. He dismissed sins. And so, in his words and deeds the cherished bedrock distinctions of human civilization—honor/shame, clean/unclean, righteousness/sin—were swept away as nothing. To those few who believed in him, his words and deeds were a revelation; they were everything.

The task today for those who would devote themselves to Jesus is to try to make these things count for something again. For centuries they have counted for little in the church. Christian civilization generally bears no mark from the ideals that shaped Jesus' message and moved his followers. Our tables are closed, our wisdom conventional, our stories self-justifying. We embrace honor and shun the shamed; we know clean from unclean, and strive to clean up our act. Discipleship is reduced to simple morality and charitable acts. The Kingdom of God is our heavenly home, or an ever-receding utopian dream that never comes any closer than the distant future. Christians believe that Jesus is God's Son. They believe in his resurrection. Oddly, we *must* believe these things to be Christian, but we need not believe *Jesus*. His words and deeds are dismissed as if they were nothing, a theological irrelevance—our scant attention to them a last vestige of wimpy nineteenth-century Liberal Theology. Of course, if we were really to give heart to Jesus' sayings today, they would affect us no less dramatically than they did his followers 2000 years ago. Believing in Jesus' resurrection costs us nothing but a penny's worth of intellectual honesty. Believing his words would cost us everything.

If Jesus is to be God's Son to anyone today, he must be so on the same terms and for the same reasons that he became the Son of God to his first followers. We must be moved by his words and deeds. This is all they had to go on. It is all we have too. Only by giving ourselves over to Jesus' ways, his ideas and ideals, will we ever know whether the thing he reveals to us is God or some other, lesser thing. This is what churches are to do. It was so from the very beginning. Churches formed as believers banded together to live out the life of Jesus; what Jesus began was continued in the Jesus movement. The church exists for discipleship. Discipleship begins with study. Jesus is its subject matter. But be careful. "If you give a mouse a cookie. . . . "

American Churches & the Culture Wars

Lane C. McGaughy

Other essays in this volume address the relevance of the work of the Jesus Seminar for the churches. The essays contribute to the larger discussion about the relationship between faith and reason. In this essay I propose to view the matter from the other side: is there something about the nature of American churches that often blocks open dialogue about the results of critical scholarship? Why are American churches and their leaders so reluctant to engage in serious debate about the implications of biblical criticism for contemporary faith? The thesis of this essay is that the separation of church and state in this country has had an unintended negative effect: it has turned churches into political action committees and ultimately made them captives to the current negative tactics being used in the culture wars between conservatives and liberals.

A Crisis of Identity

The establishment clause of the First Amendment to the Constitution of the United States has, for the most part, prevented internecine religious conflict in this country. On the other hand, it has also created an identity crisis for the many religious communities that have taken refuge under the umbrella of religious freedom guaranteed by this amendment. Prior to the American experiment in the separation of church and state, religious institutions were either state sponsored or persecuted by the state as undermining civic religion. In the European context, the sociologists Max Weber and Ernst Troeltsch used the labels "church" and

43

"sect" to distinguish these two options. Since American religious institutions have been neither supported nor opposed by the government, they are, in terms of Weber and Troeltsch's categories, neither churches nor sects. This has created an identity crisis for religious groups in America since the States ratified the First Amendment in 1791. If religious groups like Baptists and Episcopalians and Presbyterians are neither (established) churches nor (outlawed) sects, what are they?

American church historians credit Lyman Beecher (1775–1863) with coining the label "denomination" for this new American creation to distinguish it from the church and sect of its European antecedents. At first fighting against the final disestablishment of the New England churches, when the last "standing order" (the guarantee that taxpayers would underwrite church budgets) was defeated in Connecticut in 1818, Beecher decided to view the separation of the churches from state support as an opportunity to create influential voluntary movements that would transform society. According to Edward Beecher, his father's theology was "designed not only to produce revivals, but to organize society, to rally god's hosts for action, for universal conflict, and for victory in the holy war."[1] Lyman Beecher thus argued that denominations were a new utopian model for the world and the basis for a cooperative relationship between church and state.

As a result of Beecher's influence during the Second Awakening, American denominations rapidly came to be viewed as voluntary civic associations with a religious purpose or mission. Thus, the historian Sidney Mead describes a denomination as "a voluntary association of like-hearted and like-minded individuals, who are united on the basis of common beliefs for the purpose of accomplishing tangible and defined objectives."[2] Since religious denominations could no longer count on state support to guarantee funding or membership, new strategies needed to be developed to sustain denominational growth and to support their social missions. Beecher suggested two such strategies: revivalism and programmatic involvement. The first strategy was implemented in the Second Awakening during which Beecher, Charles G. Finney, and others launched a series of religious revivals through camp meetings and nightly revival services using the latest psychological techniques for persuading attendees to join their movements. The second strategy of implementing programmatic activities resulted in a burst of humanitarian institutions being created by the denominations in the nineteenth century, most notably schools, hospitals, and missionary societies. One might observe that Beecher's innovation was at least partially responsible for the later division of Protestant Christianity into fundamentalist (using the strategy of revivalism to recruit members) and liberal (enticing new members through a plethora of programmatic activities) branches. But this impulse to define religious groups as voluntary associations competing for members in a free market arena only added to the identity crisis: how are religious denominations any different from other voluntary associations in society? And why are religious associations needed to sponsor colleges, hospitals, and charitable organizations?

Denominations as Political Action Committees

The anomalous situation of religious denominations in America as being neither churches nor sects has been further compounded by a paradox: denominations have been forced to become lobbyists for their own interests in a political culture they helped to create. The sociologist Will Herberg has pointed out that we often miss the significance of the fact that the United States is a nation of immigrants. Herberg argued in his 1955 book, *Protestant-Catholic-Jew*, that this fact means that the early European immigrants to the new world all shared one feature in common, despite ethnic and linguistic differences: they all claimed the Bible as their common book. Subsequent sociologists of religion like Robert Bellah (*Religion in America*, 1968) went on to show that the ideology, rituals, and symbols of the American way of life are all derived from the biblical tradition. Thus, though the United States is legally not a Christian nation, due to the separation of church and state, it *is* a biblical nation. Stated differently, Herberg, Bellah, and others have been arguing that the Bible has functioned in two different ways in the American tradition: it is both the sacred scriptures for Protestants, Catholics, and Jews and the reservoir for the shared values and beliefs that constitute the common culture of Americans. Bellah calls this latter use of the Bible as the source for common political and cultural discourse "American civil religion."

One result of this unique history is the paradox that religious groups spawned by the Bible have had to lobby a political system deriving from the same roots to achieve the ends that European churches could mandate by virtue of their status as state-sponsored institutions. This paradox did not pose an overt problem as long as the values of Christian denominations and those of American civil religion were consistent. And this pertained so long as the Puritan worldview dominated American culture. But at least since World War II, and perhaps as early as the last great wave of immigration in the 1890s, the United States has increasingly become a pluralistic society. This means that Christian denominations can no longer assume that their values and interests will unofficially dominate secular culture. And so, religious institutions have become overt lobbying agents, forced to jockey with all the other political action committees and special interest groups for power and influence in the political arena. Mainline Christian denominations have long engaged in this attempt to influence political decisions through various church agencies, many of which are located in Washington, DC. More recently, more conservative religious groups have sponsored political action groups in a big way, mobilizing efforts to oppose abortion, gay rights, hate-crimes legislation, environmental regulations, and federal entitlements for the poor, to endorse religious activities in public schools, to support a unilateral military foreign policy, and to push through Congress other social issues they endorse. Recognizing that the legal separation of church and state places religious groups in the same category as other voluntary associations that must lobby for their own interests, many religious leaders of groups like the Moral Majority have decided to push their own ideological agendas, not by argument and persuasion, but by stocking legislative and judicial entities with persons who support those agendas. The role of religious groups as political action committees is thus now contributing to the polarization of American culture by forcing their views on the entire populace through the attempted control of legislative and judicial bodies and the extensive use of the referendum process.

The Internal Politicization of the Denominations

Most recently this strategy of using the political process to force partisan viewpoints on the wider culture has been turned against the denominations themselves. Whereas in the past dissident groups within mainline denominations would split off from a parent body if they rejected its theology or social policies, now these dissident groups are staying within denominations and trying to seize control of them through political manipulation. A case in point is the Institute on Religion and Democracy, an umbrella conservative organization that is now attempting to take control of the United Methodist Church, the Presbyterian Church (USA), and the Episcopal Church through its "Reforming America's Churches Project: 2001–2004." According to this recent funding proposal, "the IRD was founded in 1981 to combat the irresponsible political lobbying of mainline churches" (IRD: 3). But now, the funding proposal continues, the IRD is shifting from simply "countering the influence of church leaders in [sic] religious and secular elite" to proactively taking control of "the governing structures of these churches" (IRD:1) to lessen "the impact of the Religious Left" (IRD:5) on American culture.

The conservative ally of the IRD that is attempting to take control of the United Methodist Church is called the Good News movement. It has recently released a white paper called "Issues and Priorities: General Conference 2004" which describes twenty-two legislative actions intended to strip liberal influence from the UMC and replace it with conservative leadership aimed at returning the UMC to "doctrinal integrity" (GNA:1). The IRD claims that its United Methodist Action Committee was responsible for defeating pro-gay initiatives at the last General Conference of the UMC in 2000, for overturning the church's historic opposition to voluntary school prayer, and for overturning its official support of pacifism (IRD:9). The main political strategy at the moment is to reapportion the delegations to the 2004 General Conference and to change the formula for appointing members to general boards and agencies of the UMC so that more populous and conservative regions like the Southeastern Jurisdiction will gain majority control of both the legislative and administrative arenas within the UMC (GNA:11–13). If successful, the Good News movement promises to institute a doctrinal pledge for all United Methodist schools, to eliminate the Board of Church and Society in Washington, DC, to muzzle the (liberal) Women's Division, and to shift the Board of Global Ministries "away from left-wing political action and back towards traditional Christian missions" (IRD:10).

Similar wings of the IRD have formulated strategies for taking control of the Presbyterian Church (USA) and the Episcopal Church over the next several years as well. These three mainline denominations have been targeted for conservative takeover because they are deemed to be vulnerable (their memberships are declining) and because "their influence is disproportionate to their numbers" and they still control "billions of dollars" in property and endowments (IRD:1).

Denominationalism and the Culture Wars

James Davison Hunter in his analysis of the current culture wars in the United States (*Culture Wars: The Struggle to Define America*) adds one more chapter to this evolution of European churches and sects into American denominations as lobbyists for special interests in the public arena. According to Hunter (89), "religiously based special agenda organizations" have now eclipsed the denominations that spawned them as the basis of religious identification in America. As efforts to influence the larger culture through special interest advocacy groups like the Moral Majority have waxed, denominational identification and loyalty have waned, Hunter claims (87). Thus the irony now is that Lyman Beecher's effort to save the Puritan vision by turning it into voluntary associations lobbying for particular objectives is now consuming the denominations themselves. Hunter further claims that, as a result of defining denominations as advocacy groups, Beecher's proposal has led to the division of American society into two sharply opposed sides, conservatives and liberals, or, in Hunter's terms, "the orthodox and progressive impulses in American culture" (46), each of which offers competing moral visions of what the American experiment means. A corollary of Hunter's argument is his observation that, in the context of a culture war, differences are no longer settled by dialogue and negotiation, but by force. Religious advocacy groups are now competing in a political arena where no compromise is possible: the strategy is one of "deliberate, systematic effort to discredit the opposition" (136) in order to gain a total victory in the name of an absolute and nonnegotiable worldview.

Who is the Mainline Church's Audience?

In light of this description of how religious groups in the United States have evolved from European churches, to American denominations in the context of the separation of church and state, to political advocacy groups—first among the denominations and, more recently, between liberal and conservative ideologies that transcend denominational loyalties—I would like to conclude with a few, mostly personal, observations from forty years as an ordained clergyman in the Methodist Church about how perceived audiences are influencing denominational responses to these threats. In attempting to take control of mainline (=liberal) denominations, the Institute on Religion and Democracy and similar conservative movements rightly recognize that denominational executives are anxious about the decline in liberal church membership and so are, unfortunately, often vulnerable to pressures from the right. In attempting to save ecclesiastical structures and thus to preserve their own influence, many pragmatic church leaders are willing to accede to the demands of conservative lobbying groups like the Good News movement. Thus, they are increasingly caving in to demands that worship services ape those of "freeway temples," that traditional organ music and hymns be replaced with praise bands and gospel songs, and that they distance themselves from liberal movements like the Jesus Seminar. This is to assume, wrongly in my opinion, that liberal denominations are competing for the same audience as the more fundamentalist groups and so should imitate their practices. Like many others, I have argued over the years that liberal churches should be targeting a different audience: that large group of literate Americans who are disenchanted with fundamentalist views and open to the realities of the modern world. Following World War II there has been an explosion of religious studies departments in virtually every college and university in this country. This means that, for the first time, we now have a generation of Americans who have taken at least one or two academic religion courses and are open to the critical study of the Bible. Liberal denominations should take a cue from the Westar Institute and target this growing number of college-educated, professional adults who have some background in the study of religion, but who have been alienated either by the politics of "religiously based, special agenda" groups or the dogmatism of religious orthodoxy. If denominational executives were to adopt this strategy, they would not only reverse the trend of declining membership by appealing to the "church alumni association," but they would rescue liberal denominations from their current fundamentalist captivity. Such a strategy would require that mainline denominations engage in serious study of the Bible to equip their members to debate fundamentalists about its interpretation, that denominational leaders be selected from a pool of theologians and enlightened pastors rather than from the ranks of church bureaucrats and administrators, and that denominations organize national educational forums to address issues of peace, social justice, and sustainable development in such a way as to provide enlightened moral leadership in the modern world. What seems to be clear to many of us is that if liberal churches are to become healthy and authentic communities again, their fates are intimately bound up with issues of economic justice and environmental preservation. In short, liberal churches must regain their prophetic voices by freeing themselves from the intimidation of conservative pressure groups like the Institute on Religion and Democracy and the Good News movement.

Churches as Pawns in the Culture Wars

Because of their historic role as lobbying agents vis-à-vis the government, denominations were vulnerable to being used as pawns in the culture wars that erupted in the United States during the Vietnam War. Political "neoconservatives" decided that funding reactionary religious movements was one of the most effective ways to implement their conservative vision for the future of America. Leon Howell (*United Methodism @ Risk: A Wake-Up Call*) points out that funding for groups like the IRD has largely come from a handful of secular conservative corporate foundations that decided to target their philanthropy at lobbying groups who shared their social philosophy. It is thus no surprise that the rise of conservative political influence and the explosion of conservative religious lobbying efforts have occurred simultaneously in the United States since the early 1970s. In Howell's words (95), "the wider religious right has begun to focus on historic religious institutions like the Southern Baptist Convention and the mainline Protestant churches as potential allies in their prosecution of the culture wars."

The fact that conservative religious renewal groups are being directed by neoconservative political leaders and funded by conservative corporate foundations explains why the use of wedge issues has become a favorite tactic in the attempt to win control of mainline churches. Conservative renewal groups adopted this tactic from political strategists and are using three main wedge issues in their battle for control of the churches: doctrinal purity, fear of homosexuality, and opposition to abortion.[3] These are the issues that conservative action groups like the IRD's UM Action, Presbyterian Action, and Episcopal Action committees are using "to redirect these churches away from their reflexive alliance with the political left and back towards classical Christianity" (IRD:1). Given the well-organized and heavily funded attacks on the mainline churches by groups like the IRD, the work of critical biblical scholars like those in the Jesus Seminar is dismissed a priori as contrary to "Scriptural Christianity" and destructive of the "apostolic faith" of the second century which the Good News movement and other conservative action groups take to be normative for Christian faith. The efforts of the Jesus Seminar to promote biblical literacy are indeed facing stiff opposition from those who regard such work as threatening to the conservative agenda for controlling the churches.

Learning to See God
Prayer and Practice in the Wake of the Jesus Seminar

Joe Bessler-Northcutt

Introductory Parable

Kay and I were both reaching for words. "Well, it was real! They were talking about their lives, and it was so incredibly real." It was about eight years ago. We had just attended our first Sunday evening worship service at the Community of Hope and had been deeply moved by it. The Community of Hope had been established as a mission of the United Methodist Church to the gay and lesbian community through the appointment of Rev. Leslie Penrose as its minister, and was barely two years old. The "cocktail" treatments that were to prove so helpful in extending lives of men and women with AIDS were just coming on the market. By the end of their third year, they would have forty funerals. The average age of the congregation was about thirty-five. They were indeed dealing with real things that night. Several young men were in wheelchairs, some with oxygen tanks at their sides. No one was dressed up. There were about forty of us in all, squeezing into our metal chairs around a small room.

Still, the mood was bright. They sang of being "companions on the journey"; we got the hang of it by verse three. The centerpiece of the service was "joys and concerns"—a portion of worship unlike anything I had ever heard. There was no, "Lord, we ask you," as members of the group talked about their lives, no "hear our prayer" at the end. Just silence as we took in one concern after another, except for the joys, which that night were hysterically funny, perhaps because we needed them to be. At one point, a young man told of trying to talk to his father about being gay. His father had become furious and had almost physically thrown him out of the house. As he told us about it, he rolled his eyes and spit an expletive with a laugh that held his dignity. We laughed, too, but held our breath at the pain of it. Another man asked us to celebrate with him in marking a year of sobriety. The group cheered. A woman in her early thirties asked us to pray for her. She had been "clean" for six months and had started "using" again. We were still, and those near her put their arms around her. A young man's dog, a beautiful "lab" that had been "with me for nine years" was missing. Another's mom had been diagnosed with colon cancer.

Several founding members of the Community were in the hospital that night. Leslie told stories of visiting with them—of their honest fears, of their longings for acceptance from a home church or just from home, of their anger in rejecting the beliefs of the church (whichever one it was) that had rejected them.

They also celebrated communion that night as they do each week, it turned out. A Community of Hope communion is a rather raucous event. There was very little traditional piety as folks sang, laughed, talked, and hugged one another while approaching the bread and the cup. Kay and I were hugged as well, thanked for attending, and kidded about something even as Michael said, "The Bread of Life," "Amen." and Glenda said, "Hi! The Cup of Hope," "Amen."

And Leslie preached. Picking up fragments of the night's joys and concerns, and weaving them into the gospel story—the woman with a hemorrhage. She talked about the Community and its resistance to a church and a culture that not only ignored but frequently despised them. She talked about the way of Jesus and the healing involved in the woman's restoration to community. And she talked about being an inclusive community that reached out to others: reminding them of their commitment to the homeless, of their work in establishing Hope House to provide housing to those dying with AIDS or to house women trying to get off the streets, and of spending a dollar outside the church for every dollar they took in. The Community of Hope was not to be a ghetto, but a place that practiced the vision it sought. Nor could the Community simply be about "church" in some private sense; it had to be about changing society as well—its attitudes but also its structures.

One seldom hears the kind of honesty, or the kind of joy, we heard that night, let alone in the midst of worship. Intended or not we felt its attraction as an invitation we could not refuse. And our lives the eight years since that night have not been the same. In part, because of my connection to the Community of Hope I have learned to see God—differently. Still, I credit not only the Community of Hope but also my colleagues of the Jesus Seminar for bringing me to a point of answerability, of owning with confidence a vision of the Christian faith that stands in critical tension with the traditions both religious and secular that have shaped me. It has taken time for me to own my skepticism toward my traditions as something other than my problem, and to see it as a creative and public resource for re-imagining Christian faith.[1]

Skepticism and Christology

The ability to acknowledge one's skepticism as a creative resource rather than as a point of shame is vital to re-imagining Christian prayer and practice in the wake of the Jesus Seminar.[2] In his 1968 essay, "Contemplation in a World of Action," Thomas Merton argued that "official contemplative life as it is lived in our monasteries needs a great deal of rethinking, because it is still too closely identified with patterns of thought that were accepted five hundred years ago, but which are completely strange to modern man (sic)."[3] Moreover:

> Experience of the contemplative life in the modern world shows that the most crucial focus for contemplative and meditative discipline, and for the life of prayer, for many modern men (sic), is precisely this so-called sense of absence, desolation, and even apparent 'inability to believe.' I stress the word 'apparent,' because though this experience may to some be painful and confusing, raising all kinds of crucial 'religious problems,' it can very well be a sign of authentic Christian growth and a point of decisive development in faith, if they are able to cope with it. The way to cope with it is not to regress to an earlier and less mature stage of belief, to stubbornly reaffirm and to 'enforce' feelings, aspirations and images that were appropriate to one's childhood and first communion. One must, on a new level of meditation and prayer, live through this crisis of belief and grow to a more personal and Christian integration of experience.[4]

In this essay, I look to the sayings and parables of Jesus to provide both a warrant and a model for the kind of skepticism that discloses resources for renewing Christian thought, prayer, and practice.

Merton's "crisis of belief" is perhaps nowhere more apparent than in discussions of christology. As that subdiscipline of Christian theology where one speaks most forcefully of God-with-us, christological preoccupation with Jesus' metaphysical identity, (i.e., as second person of the Trinity, as divine incarnation, as atoning for all the sins of humanity in his death and his resurrection) utterly overlooked not only the life and teaching of Jesus, but also the problem of discerning the immanence of God in *our* human lives. To the modern person the metaphysical assumptions behind the traditional, doctrinal claims about Jesus appear simply and utterly mythological. Critical of the cosmological, political, and gender assumptions that shaped traditional language about the nature of God and the world, of sin and Christ, etc., scholars have developed a wide variety of approaches designed to help people of faith re-imagine the reality of God. Ecological and new cosmological theologies, hermeneutical theologies, political and liberation, feminist and womanist theologies—are all engaged in the critical rethinking of Christian traditions that stem from the emergence of intellectual disciplines and political practices that have utterly reshaped our cultural assumptions about reality.

My interest in historical-Jesus research stems from my conviction that theologians need to re-imagine the core area of christology so that Christians might learn to see differently not only Jesus, but also God. The turning point in challenging more traditionalist christologies occurred with the recognition by biblical scholars that Jesus did not in all probability claim to be God. Nor did he claim that *he* was the focus of his teaching.[5] Rather, his preoccupation was with the Kingdom of God, which he saw occurring in the midst of the world.[6] While I take seriously the tradition's claim that christology provides the key discussion for exploring the reality of God-with-us, it is important to shift the meaning of "christology" away from the tradition's emphasis on Jesus' metaphysical identity. Such claims fail to move a contemporary audience because of their unintelligibility and patriarchal character. Instead, christology should illuminate the kind of social dynamics to which Jesus pointed when he spoke of the Kingdom of God. In that way, the "Christ," which is to say, the human experience of the immanence of God, is normed by Jesus' discourse of the Kingdom.

A Rhetorical Jesus

Evident to even the casual reader of the gospels is that Jesus was not a philosopher in the style of Plato or Aristotle, i.e., arguing from first principles. Instead, Jesus used the conventions of Israel's religious and cultural heritage. What I have found most helpful in the Jesus Seminar's attempt to sift the Jesus traditions for words and acts most probably his own is the emergent sense of a rhetorical voice engaging the available conventions of its first-century audience. Other scholars outside the seminar have moved in a similar direction.

Richard Horsely, for example, suggests Jesus engaged in local projects of community building—helping peasant families and workers to resist the shame and worthlessness with which the taxation, farming policies, and religious purity codes labeled them. Set within the social world of first-century Mediterranean peasant culture, Jesus' rhetoric of the Kingdom of God was not about a new kingdom about to be imposed from beyond the world by God.[7] Rather, in his language of the Kingdom, or Empire, of God, Jesus urged his audience to be that kind of community where God's presence and not Rome's presence was fully established, to live out of Israel's prophetic vocation to seek justice for everyone—even one's enemy—to welcome the stranger, and thus to see God in ways that violated the myth and mores of the dominant culture. Writing about life in the villages of the Galilee, Horsely comments:

> Unfortunately, under the pressure of debt and taxation, Roman legal standards, not the Torah, began to take precedence. Villagers who may previously have felt responsibility to help their neighbors in times of shortage were no longer under legal obligation to do so, especially since they were themselves now debtors, hard-pressed to provide their own children with food to eat. Local feuds which could have been easily resolved in normal times now often erupted into insults, fistfights, and family feuds. Land or goods taken as loan collateral—that should have been returned to its original owners by the law of the sabbatical year— now became the big-city creditors' permanent property. The simple fact was that the People of Israel were badly divided. Villagers who should have cooperated in their own liberation were at each others' throats. Jesus' healings and teachings must be therefore seen in this context, not as abstract spiritual truths spoken between stunning miracles but as a program of community action and practical resistance to a system that efficiently transformed close-knit villages into badly fragmented communities of alienated, frightened individuals.[8]

While Stephen Patterson doesn't see exactly what Horsley has called a "program of community renewal" in the sayings, parables, and miracles of Jesus, he also sees Jesus addressing the social world of the villages, especially the situation of those anthropologist G. Lenski termed "expendables." Writing about the cultural effects of the Roman patronage system, Patterson describes their situation.

> In a patronage system, those who have nothing to offer someone above them gradually fall through the cracks in the bottom of the system. . . . These are the beggars and the homeless. These

are persons who might do those jobs no one else would do, like
tax collecting. These are persons who count for nothing, like
prostitutes. With so many people living at the margins of existence, a significant number of expendables was always an
inevitability, with persons moving in and out of that status all
the time. Take, for example, the situation of agricultural day
laborers. If they are fortunate enough to get a full day's work, then
they will receive enough pay to eat for a day. That is what subsistence means. . . . For a peasant living at a subsistence level,
expendability is only one day away.[9]

Patterson sees Jesus as undermining the cultural assumptions of
clean/unclean, shame/honor, and sin/righteousness in order to affirm the
human dignity of expendables and to insist on a model of human community—call it the Kingdom of God—that welcomed expendables as full
participants.[10] While Patterson may overdo the use of "existential" language, which can suggest a more individual rather than communal or public focus, his chief concerns are communal and ethical in ways that
complement Horsley's approach.

In Jesus' language of the Kingdom of God, the emphasis falls not on
the kingly character of God, (i.e., God as King) but on the social space,
(i.e., the kingdom) within which the reality of God is experienced.[11] By
characterizing that social space of the kingdom in the terms of the marginalized and fragmented world of peasant villages, Jesus rhetorically
shifted the *location* of God's experienced presence, templizing, in effect,
his audience's sphere of human experience in order to reinvigorate both
their sense of worth and their sense of responsibility for enacting that
social space of the Kingdom of God. Jesus' rhetorical relocation of Israel's
God-language functioned ironically not only to critique, or lampoon, the
legitimacy of Roman power, but also to summon the people of these villages to respond more deeply to their vocation of being a people of God.[12]
It would not be enough for his peasant, largely Jewish audience to mock
Rome in a kind of foolish Jewish nationalism. Rather they would have to
do some soul searching, skeptical not only of the cultural assumptions that
belittled them, but skeptical as well about their own participation, their
own enforcement of those oppressive mores against their neighbors.[13]
Renewal would require new habits of seeing and new habits of acting.

In the following section, I explore the creative balance of skepticism
and hope in several of Jesus' parables and sayings. I will then suggest how
the dynamic at work in those parables can enable us to practice a twenty-
first century skepticism of Christian traditions with hope for renewing and
transforming the practices of Christian thought and prayer.

Parables and Sayings

In the sayings and parables that I examine below, the issue of "seeing" is important both to the action of the parable and to its effects on Jesus' audience. The concern with "sight" in these parables is not the same as the desire for epistemological foundationalism that Richard Rorty criticized in *Philosophy and the Mirror of Nature*.[14] Rather, the parables' metaphorical concerns with "seeing" tend to work in the direction of skepticism, of breaking down the peasants' assumptions about the sacred and political organization of their world while opening up alternative ways of seeing and acting. In his sayings and parables, Jesus enabled his hearers to acknowledge not only their own skepticism but also their agency, their responsibility, to embrace different assumptions about participation in the human community.

A Good Samaritan

In this story of a Jewish man, beaten, robbed, and stripped of his clothing and dignity, Jesus turns the economic frustrations of his hearers first onto Israel's religious elite and then onto themselves. Christians have tended to see in the Samaritan the figure of Christian gentiles, who, in doing out of love what the Jewish authorities failed to do because of the Law, surpassed the Jewish covenant. What the Christian view fails to account for, however, is Jesus' own audience, and what they would have heard. Scott has reminded readers of the importance of the wounded man's nakedness—that apart from clothing that would indicate social class, the man becomes truly anonymous.[15] Thus, neither the priest, nor Levite, nor Samaritan could know the identity of the wounded Jewish man in the ditch. By having the figures of the Jewish priest and Levite both see and pass by the wounded man, however, Jesus prompted the skeptical question of whether purity and legal obligations fully enact the life that Israel should lead. In fact, the parable suggests that knowledge of the Law can enable the denial of the educated and priestly classes, blinding them to the more basic and urgent need of acknowledging their neighbor.[16] However, Jesus did not leave the ethics of peasant Jews alone either. While initially encouraging peasant suspicions of the literate classes, Jesus' use of the Samaritan as hero skeptically asks whether anyone else in his audience would have acted differently from the priest or Levite.[17] In other words, the parable indicts all of Israel for failing to do what it knows it ought to do. As the parable makes painfully obvious, even a Samaritan can "see" what needs to be done, and even worse, the Samaritan does it before the Jew. Thus, the parable urged an acknowledgment on the part of Jesus' audience that possessing the Law, the Temple, the Sabbath—whatever revelation one wanted to tout as marking one's superiority and

uniqueness—was of no advantage if one used them to deny the fundamental moral imperatives of caring for those in need. By calling the ulti-
macy of those traditions and cultural possessions into question, Jesus left
no boundary between the Jew and the Samaritan and thus no boundary to
the Kingdom of God.

Considering Lilies

"Consider the lilies, how they grow; they neither toil nor spin, yet I
tell you, even Solomon in all his glory was not clothed as one of these."
The saying, taken from Q, is found in both Matthew (6:28b–29) and in
Luke (12:27). According to the Seminar fellows, it is part of what may be
"the longest connected discourse that can be directly attributed to Jesus,"
excepting some of the longer parables.[18] The verse is part of a broader discourse addressing anxiety about basic bodily needs, and is addressed "to
those who are preoccupied with day-to-day existence."[19] So, verse 25 in
Matthew: "Therefore I tell you do not worry about your life, what you will
eat or about what you will drink, or about your body, what you will wear.
Is not life more than food, and the body more than clothing?"

Gentler than the story of the Samaritan, Jesus' sayings here also
encouraged his favored, peasant audience to be somewhat skeptical of
their own anxieties for the sake of a bigger picture. The preoccupation
with bodily needs, suggested Jesus, could prevent one from "seeing" what
is really needed, namely justice. Obsessed with pursuing those basic needs,
one might trade away one's dignity, becoming a virtual slave to, and for,
food. Alternatively, the preoccupation with survival needs could enable a
kind of denial about the other real needs of life, such as community,
mutual regard, and forgiveness. Insofar as poverty tears at the basic fabric
of community by pitting the destitute against one another, isolating them
by their competition for scarce resources, the parable urged his hearers to
remember that that behavior could not grow a community, much less the
Kingdom of God. By turning to examples from nature, (e.g., the lilies of
the field and the birds of the air), Jesus encouraged his listeners to "see"
an integrity set apart from any economic, political, or religious power to
shame. Arguing from the convention that God provides for the creatures
of the earth, Jesus urged a constructive confidence in place of a destructive anxiety. "Seek first the Kingdom of God."

If, by the phrase "Kingdom of God," Jesus meant living as a *just* community—even in the face of Roman occupation—then both ruling elites
and peasants would need the courage to be skeptical about *their* interests—purity and law on the one hand, and survival needs on the other. A
just village would resist the moral corruption of Roman occupation by
refusing to treat one another as the Romans had hoped they would.

Hiding Leaven

In this parable Jesus shifts the assumption of God's active location from "purity" to "impurity," leaving some in his audience reassured, according to Scott, while leaving others quite upset.

> For all those who are leaven in their society, this parable assures them that the empire of God is like them. In Jesus' society this was a large majority of the people. All those who were unable for one reason or another to observe the purity code would be leaven and that would be most folks. . . .
>
> Of course, for all those who were doing well under the current regime, this parable would be bad news. God was not like what they imagined or the scriptures had predicted. God was not like unleavened bread, but leavened. The boundary of the sacred established by the Feast of Unleavened Bread is eliminated.[20]

Leaven, associated with the processes of decomposition and rot, accomplishes in nature what skepticism achieves in discourse—the dismantling of what seems true, pure, and whole. That Jesus associates the Kingdom of God with that corrupting process suggests again a scandalous relocation of the divine presence. Just as the woman's act of hiding the leaven suggests the secretive act of "concealing," so Jesus may have commented here on the hidden presence of God, concealed precisely where one's cultural and religious assumptions forbade such presence. Here as before, Jesus encouraged a skepticism toward the basic cultural assumptions of clean-and-unclean to make plain the terribly difficult but more fundamental obligation to affirm and care for everyone in the community.

An Always Final Judgment

While the story of the final judgment in Matthew 25:31–46 is considered by vote of the Jesus Seminar almost certainly the construction of Matthew, I believe it is profoundly in sync with Jesus' own religious vision. Matthew uses an eschatological framework to focus his readers' attention about the nature of wisdom. At the heart of the parable are persons both saved and damned who did not recognize the king who was to judge them. In fact, response of those who are saved because "I was hungry and you gave me food, naked and you clothed me . . . " is "but when did we see you hungry and give you food. . . . " The king tells them, "As often as you did this to one of the least of these, my family, you did this to me." As framed by the story, salvation is not dependent on one's attendance at synagogue or Temple, or even on possessing the right theology. Instead, the king's own presence is placed in the midst of impurity and utter deprivation, requiring not knowledge but acknowledgment. Yet, as with those who are damned, if one thought that blindness might be an excuse, the parable rather laboriously points out this is not the case. Failure to recognize the king in the homeless and the hungry is no excuse for those who failed to offer the cup of water. Even if they had possessed true theological knowledge of the eschatological judge, it would be of no advantage if they failed to attend to the king's hidden presence. As in the stories of the lily and of the Good Samaritan, the presence of God occurs where one least expects—directly in sight, under one's nose, in the midst of those most anxious about possessing basic things and fulfilling basic human desires.

By surprising both the saved and the damned, the parable again prompts skepticism toward those institutions, and their leaders, that provide more legalistic, ritualistic, or theoretical means to salvation that enable one to sidestep one's responsibility to the neighbor in need. Simultaneously, the story prompts those listening to seek God in that more troublesome space of human need.

Taking Jesus Seriously

It may seem strange to discuss the role of skepticism in Jesus' parables in an essay that attempts to talk about prayer. I am convinced, however, that persons or Christian communities that have no capacity for skepticism about their traditions, (and there are *many* communities like this), will be unable to integrate the research and findings of the Jesus Seminar into their personal lives or corporate life of prayer and practice. By underscoring the creative role of skepticism in opening the religious imagination of Jesus' audiences, I hope to provide a powerful warrant and model for acknowledging the legitimate role of skepticism in the life of a tradition. Insofar as Jesus' sayings and parables make painfully clear what is needed for peasant, Jewish villages to act with integrity and faith in the face of Roman aggression, they do not dismiss the reality of the sacred, but relocate it as a summons for both courage and hope. By combining, in uncanny ways, these dynamics of skepticism and hope, the parables— and the relocation of God they affect—remain important resources for responding to the crisis of faith Merton described almost forty years ago.

How might taking Jesus' relocation of God in the parables help us to relocate the significance of prayer and religious ritual in our lives? It is fitting, I think, to begin with that wonderfully skeptical line that Peter O'Toole's character utters in the film, *The Ruling Class*: "I *must* be God. Every time I pray, I find I'm talking to myself." The character's conclusion is funny precisely because it names the audience's own, frequently hidden, skepticism about their own experience of prayer.

Like Jesus' hearers, I believe we need to learn to see God differently.[21] I believe that our tendency to equate faith with ascent to the doctrinal claims of the Christian tradition actually enables our blindness to the call of Jesus' gospel. Locked in models of prayer, both corporate and private, that accentuate the image of an omnipotent, supreme being living beyond the world, to whom we humbly "lift our minds and hearts," we fail to "see" the presence of God in the midst of public life.[22] And so we equate holiness with going to church instead of going to work, and we view our obligation to God in private and cultic ways that narrow and misshape our responsibility as persons for one another. Almost inevitably, religious traditions and their leaders become convinced of their own importance, justify their power by their possession of eternal truth as the only refuge from human sinfulness, and discourage skepticism as a sign of pride and sin. Unable to own our skepticism, we are in need of contemporary parables, some of them like the Community of Hope, to encourage a skepticism that opens onto a more creative path.

In light of contemporary cosmology and our ethical rejection of imperial, colonial, and patriarchal forms of human (and divine) governance, it is time to reject Christianity's traditional theistic language of God (i.e., imagining God as a Supreme Being with a divine mind and a divine will that controls all things, etc.). Instead we need theologies that leaven that traditional image and relocate the primary experience of God to the midst of public life, a move that calls us to live up to and pursue that elusive longing for a just and compassionate society to which Jesus pointed. Acknowledging with the parable of the Samaritan that Jews, Buddhists, and others see and do what we, as Christians, with all our truth, fail to see and do, we now need more desperately than ever to leaven those boundaries of salvation that distinguish between privileged insiders and dismissible outsiders.

In relocating God from the truth claims of the church into the experienced practices of justice and compassion in public life, I don't mean to dismiss Christian traditions as much as caution against taking them as the final norms of Christian life. By relocating the primary presence of God to the world of public life, I hope to return some sense of mystery, sacrality, and gravitas to the public realm and to our shared responsibility for it. Resisting what Scott has called the "default" ethics of cultural self-assurance and complacency, the parables and sayings of Jesus call us to experience God in the complex yet basic work of building more just communities.

If we begin to think of the presence of God in such public terms then we will need to re-imagine our understanding of prayer and worship too.

Thomas Merton's own transition from the otherworldly spirituality of *The Seven Storey Mountain* (1948) to the embrace of the world in his later writings can be instructive for us. In *Conjectures of a Guilty Bystander* (1966), Merton wrote:

> In Louisville, at the corner of Fourth and Walnut, in the center of the shopping district, I was suddenly overwhelmed with the realization that I loved all those people, that they were mine and I theirs, that we could not be alien to one another even though we were total strangers. It was like waking from a dream of separateness, of spurious self-isolation in a special world, the world of renunciation and supposed holiness. The whole illusion of a separate holy existence is a dream.[23]

Merton's 1971 essay, "Contemplation in a World of Action," continues his attempt to shift the language of Christian contemplation from escape to engagement.[24] Here one can see the attempt to overcome the dualities of sacred and profane, of the monastery and the world. So for us the practice of private, personal prayer can become a time in which we rehearse, not flee from, the desires and motivations that shape our participation in public life. Just as the presence of God shifts in this model from imperial subject to public process, so prayer that attends to God will be attentive, nurturing the values of public life: of respect that is open to being changed by the other, of hospitality that welcomes the stranger, of compassion that preserves the dignity of one's enemies, of skepticism toward our own, as well as others' interests, of anger in the face of injustice against persons, and in our time especially, as well, against the earth. In the tradition of prayer as attention: stillness, study, and reflection are all vital practices for rehearsing and deepening our experience of God encountered in the world.[25]

With respect to church participation, one might well ask, "If God is encountered *primarily* in the world and not in the church, then what is the purpose of belonging to a church community?" Simply put, the point is *practice*. Practice hospitality, practice respect, practice humility, practice conversation and disagreement, practice being community—practice the disciplines of being a public body—so that we can grow in embodying and enacting the virtues of public life in a way that challenges and inspires others as well.

Imagine the difference in one's perception of being a "greeter" at one's church on Sunday morning if one approached the task as practicing the virtue of hospitality *so that* one might better live that virtue throughout the range of one's public life. Or imagine the difference in one's perception of Communion—of the Table—if one viewed it as a practice of community *so that* one might better live the virtues of respect and equal regard in the rest of one's public life, expecting to see and commune with the mystery of God in all of those public spaces. Such an understanding of Church would give real purpose to our being there. It would underscore the reality that God is met in the public life of the world, and that the church should be a sacrament of that transforming presence. Moreover, the church is the place and the community within which we practice the vulnerability of trying—and frequently failing—to become the people that God calls us to be.[26]

In its broad-ranging, and lengthy, ritual of joys and concerns, the Community of Hope rehearses the work of carrying one another's burdens by taking the time to listen to one another's lives. Perhaps it is a sacrament of attentive listening, or of conversation. What I experience in that process of joys and concerns is a ritual of *being* a community. It is not simply a recitation of needs, but a meeting of eyes, the touch of hands, expressions of real joy and utter despair, that all acknowledge our accountability to one another. In the process, week in and week out, we celebrate the presence of God in our midst, and encourage one another to see that presence elsewhere in our lives and to seize it for the sake of a just community.

Conclusion

While I suspect there are a variety of ways in which the publications and the insights of the Jesus Seminar can be introduced into contemporary mainline churches, I am skeptical of *any* short-run transformation of contemporary Christianity. Various denominations—even with strong wings opposing resurgent fundamentalist and ultra-orthodox influences—are largely too anxious about their falling numbers and dwindling cultural influence to risk additional losses at the hands of theological reform. Nonetheless, I think that Westar's public approach and itinerant workshops participate with other voices in leavening Christian communities, encouraging a skepticism toward outmoded and patriarchal traditions bent only on securing the truth claims of the past. The process has begun; the whole batch will be leavened; and that will be a good thing, at least in parables of the Kingdom of God.

The Search for Community
& the Historical Jesus

Hal Taussig

Primary role of Jesus Seminar = nurture of community

This essay is meant as a companion to three previous essays written for the Jesus Seminar concerning the contemporary significance of the historical Jesus.[1] In this essay I want to assess how much (or little) portraits of the historical Jesus can contribute to a primary role of churches in contemporary America. That primary role is/would be the promotion and nurture of community.

The Problem of Individualism and the Need for Community in America Today

In a recent, coauthored book, *Re-Imagining Life Together in America: A New Gospel of Community*, I have described what I call "the American disaster" of over-individualization and lack of community in the following way: *ask Elaine*

Jennifer lives alone in a gated community outside St. Louis, Missouri. 27 years old, she is single and enjoys her apartment and job. She works from 8 a.m to 6 p.m. in health care administration, a position she took four years ago after graduation from college in Minnesota. Her family lives in a working class suburb on the east coast. She has made some friends at work and keeps in regular telephone contact with college friends and family. She works out three times a week at a health club, and goes to church about once a month. She has had one serious sexual relationship

what to missing?
p 68

while in Missouri, but is currently unattached. Her car, which is essential to her life, is 18 months old.

The rhythm of her life is relatively stable. Her work and exercise routine takes up most of her time during the week. She usually gets home between 7 and 9 p.m.—depending on her exercise routine—grabs something to eat in front of the TV, and goes to bed. On weekends she does some exercise, watches some more TV, does some shopping, and sees a friend or goes to church. She likes to travel for vacation, and also will occasionally visit her family or college friends on a long weekend.

On the one hand, Jennifer's life is right out of a flashy commercial for a new car. She has almost everything Americans want. Freedom to lead her own life, money to treat herself regularly, and good looks are in ample supply. As her likeness to the commercial indicates, she is not far from the American ideal. On the other hand, there is a haunting quality to Jennifer's life style. What she lacks is community. The way her life represents both a cultural ideal and an almost complete lack of in-depth connections to any group illustrates what this chapter understands as "the American disaster."

With some variation Jennifer's life is like many Americans overall, and very similar to what many others would like their life to be. It may not be that everyone can afford membership in a health club, but the growth of that industry indicates that there is still a growing market for it. The amount of TV Jennifer watches actually may be less than most Americans, but her gravitation toward it in non-working moments is almost archetypal to the contemporary American psyche. The priority she gives to a good-paying job and the consequent geographic distance of her friends and family is not exceptional. Her non-married status now represents the majority of Americans. Although most Americans do not live alone, more and more do, and the number of persons in living units steadily declines. That Jennifer goes shopping more often than to church or any social or cultural club is typical.

Whether the many Americans whose lifestyles resemble Jennifer are "happy" is not easy to answer. The direct correspondence between the rise in alcoholism, drug addiction, and depression and the emergence of this life style cannot be the sole indicator in responding to such a question, but certainly heightens the question itself. The increase in violence and anti-social behavior in America might be related to this increased lack of community. Provisionally, one can at least note some obvious personal down sides to this life style without necessarily identifying the exact causal relationships . . . Robert Putnam (noted sociologist) does believe there is a connection between the lack of community and these signs of "unhappiness."

A recent interview with retired baseball superstar Mike Schmidt illustrates this malaise beneath the surface of American affluence and individualism. About a visit back to the major league dugout, Schmidt says: "When I walked into the coaches' room, they looked at me as enjoying a life they'd probably rather have, given the choice. Financially, I don't have to keep a steady job. But I'm looking at them thinking, 'What a great life you've got. . . . ' I'm not sure what I'm going to do in the morning when I wake up. Sometimes I'm bored or stressed out from just talking on the phone, not sure what I'm going to do. I get migraines. . . . I don't feel a lot of substance in my life. It's like I'm living my life just for me."

What catapults this community-less life style into the category of an "American disaster" are not just its complex connections to personal "unhappiness" but its social, economic, cultural, and ecological consequences. The relative "unhappiness" of such community-less persons is one thing. The effect of this life style on the society, millions of people around the world, and earth itself makes up the heart of the disaster.

The mobile American individualist is a cornerstone for the huge discrepancies in income levels among Americans. The tendency of so many of us to live like Jennifer decreases understanding in American society by isolating us from one another. The huge dependency on oil, cheap labor around the world, and a national servant class—all produced by our mobility and isolated living units—are intimately and complexly related to growing social strains and violence. The devastating consumption of natural resources from both our country and around the globe by Americans—whether they be affluent corporate executives or addicted Walmart shoppers—has already changed the climate of earth itself and has resulted in the largest extermination of species in the history of the planet.

Adding to the disastrous character of this life style is the completely paradoxical public image it has. As noted earlier, this life—so devoid of community, so conducive to depression and addiction, and so destructive of social connectedness and environmental wellness—is held up as the ideal for which Americans should strive.

Perhaps most curiously, none of these observations about the disastrous consequences of our lack of community in America is new. Many of these American anti-communitarian character traits were noticed almost 200 years ago by the visiting French writer, Alexis de Tocqueville. More recently, in the past 15 years, a number of American historians and sociologists have described in great detail both the major causes and consequences of the American lack of community. The works of Robert N. Bellah, Robert Wuthnow, and Robert D. Putnam form the centerpiece of this new attention to America's lack of community. (137–39)

Churches and the Lack of American Community

Catherine Nerney and I in *Re-Imagining Life Together in America* propose that "churches in America are strategically located to help Americans claim a sense of community belonging." (xv) Although our work is the first to make this case in book-length, we are not the first to assert this. The last twenty years of work by sociologist Robert Bellah, the last ten by best-selling Harvard sociologist Robert Putnam, the Saguaro Center on Civic Engagement at Harvard, the Roper Center for Political Opinion Research at the University of Connecticut, and the DDB World Wide Survey of Chicago all have made similar suggestions.

For instance, Putnam asserts that "faith communities in which people worship together are arguably the single most important repository of social capital in America." (66) He further shows that "nearly half of all associational memberships in America are church related, half of all personal philanthropy is religious in character, and half of all volunteering occurs in a religious context." (66) For Putnam, however, it is not just that "America is one of the most religiously observant countries in the contemporary world," but rather that churches effectively shape a wide range of peoples' lives toward community.

Regular worshippers and people who say that religion is very important to them are much more likely than other people to visit friends, to entertain at home, to attend club meetings, and to belong to sports groups; professional and academic societies; school service groups; youth groups; service clubs; hobby or

garden clubs; literary, art, discussion and study groups; school fra-
ternities and sororities; farm organizations; political clubs;
nationality groups; and other miscellaneous groups. (67)

Furthermore,

agree?

religiously active men and women learn to give speeches, run
meetings, manage disagreements, and bear administrative responsibility. They also befriend others who are in turn likely to recruit
them into other forms of community activity. (66)

Although Robert Bellah's pivotal 1986 collective volume *Habits of
the Heart: Individualism and Commitment in American Life* only briefly considered the role of churches in the formation of American community, his
subsequent work has emphasized the pivotal role churches do and can play
in the crucial formation of community for Americans. He proposed in
1998:

THE BEST CHURCH COMMUNITY

I think we have to seriously consider religious community since
it is the best community at a local level, provided we can encourage each other through that community to think about the problems that are facing us in the larger society, not at the expense of
spirituality, but out of an understanding of who we are as a people of God. (11)

For Bellah, it is not that the churches are perfect, it is rather,

that I have less confidence in anything else. The local parish or
congregation is for many people in this society the only voluntary group that connects them to the larger society . . . (10)

Robert Putnam illustrates the sustaining power of church attendance
in giving people a sense of belonging and even happiness. In examining
the leading activities that gave people the most "happiness" (volun-
teerism, club meetings, entertaining people at home), Putnam found that
most activities done in moderation made people happier. Putnam found,
however, no such trend in church going. There was no limit to the
increase of happiness as one increased one's relationship to church. Of
those surveyed in the nationally recognized DDB Needham Life Style
study, the more one attended church the happier one was.
"Churchgoing...is somewhat different, in that at least up through weekly
attendance, the more the merrier," Putnam concludes. (334)[2]

First-Century Christianity and Community Formation

One of the main characteristics of first-century Christianity is its fascination with and ability to form community. That early Christians were excited about their lives together in community encourages us in our efforts to learn to live together today. The Acts of the Apostles, written around the end of Christianity's first century expresses this excitement this way: "The whole group of believers was united, heart and soul; no one claimed private ownership of any possessions, as everything they owned was held in common." (4:32) A closer look at the way early Christian groups emerged reveals even more promise. Not only is the early Christian affirmation of community resonant. The way these groups came into being can be examined in enough detail to help identify some instructive hallmarks of their existence. Although no models from one historical era can be completely transposed to another time, the study of early Christian communities' development has advanced enough to make certain patterns from that time available as exciting examples for our time.

The very earliest documents we have from Christians are the letters of Paul in the early 50s CE to a variety of groups in what is now Turkey, Rome, and Greece. Although we know that Jesus of Nazareth lived in the northern territories of colonial Israel prior to these letters and that in that territory there were probably some written documents at least from the same period as Paul, the letters of Paul to those groups are our earliest complete testimonies to some kind of Christian movement. In the letters Paul makes clear that some of the groups already existed before he knew them, some of them he was instrumental in founding, and some of them he had not yet even met. From this, scholars have concluded that these first Christian groups in Turkey, Greece, Syria and Rome most likely came into being in the 40s and early 50s CE.

A closer look at these earliest Christian documents surprises the reader with their interest in community. Paul's letters contain only one very short story about Jesus and only one paragraph of teaching reported as coming from Jesus. In all of Paul's correspondence with these groups there seems to be little interest in the deeds and teachings of Jesus of Nazareth.

Instead, the letters brim with messy negotiations about the groups' social dynamics. They are full of debates and reflections on how the group members relate to one another. The letters discuss extensively who should talk when the group gets together (e.g. 1 Cor 11–14); how Jews and gentiles should act toward one another (Galatians 2 and 3; Philippians 3, Romans 14); how slaves and masters should relate in the group

(Philemon); the character of male-female relations (1 Corinthians 11, 14); what joining the group means (Rom 6:1–11); where the group should shop (1 Corinthians 8 and 10); who should be leaders in the group (1 Thessalonians 1, 3; Romans 1, 1 Corinthians 2 – 4); sexual conduct (1 Thessalonians 4, 1 Corinthians 6, 7), and what the groups should do with their money (Philippians 1, Romans 15). The letters make constant reference to various personalities in the respective communities, cajoling some, greeting others heartily, and contesting with still others. Who God in Christ is for them is inseparable from their particular community dynamics.

An underlying and central agenda of these letters is the character and quality of people's life in community. In the back-and-forth of Paul's rhetoric one can see group identities being forged and negotiated as the communities work painstakingly on issue after issue. And although Paul's perspective often pushes each community to be in agreement with him, the way Paul writes also reveals both that his viewpoint did not always prevail and that the communities were often quite different from one another. What the correspondence has in common is the conviction that the character of community life matters greatly both for Paul and for those to whom he writes. Paul and these communities cannot conceive of an abstract, non-communal message about God.[3]

This applies not only to the letters of Paul but to the composition of the gospels and other letters and books both in and outside what eventually became Christian canon.

Biblical scholars of the last thirty years have begun to produce portraits of the communities that composed the books of the New Testament. We can now much more easily imagine who the people were who wrote and inspired the New Testament. Using the methodologies of anthropology and sociology alongside more traditional New Testament disciplines, scholars are attempting to draw initial pictures of what these early communities looked like.

This research is so widespread and complicated that even a cursory review is impossible. Three striking book-length portraits of early Christian communities do, however, serve as examples of this major new dimension to New Testament scholarship in the past thirty years. The Roman Catholic biblical scholar, Raymond Brown, produced in 1979 one of the first such books, *The Community of the Beloved Disciple*, a nuanced description of the several different groups that composed the Gospel of John and the three Epistles of John. Making deft use of what is known as rhetorical criticism, Antoinette Wire less than a decade after Brown was able to draw a portrait of the Corinthian community to which Paul wrote in her *The Corinthian Women Prophets*. Most popular and at the same time most sophisticated in methodology is *The Lost Gospel: Q and Christian Origins* by Burton L. Mack (1995), which pictures how some of the first generation of Galileans after Jesus lived and worked together. Although these portraits cannot be seen as definitive, neither the attractiveness of their historical sketches nor the sophistication of their research method-ology can be denied.[4] This very methodology has already shown that the attention to community by early Christians and their own successes in building community was not necessarily because of some particular virtue of them or their message. Indeed, it is clear that early Christians drew upon both larger and newly emerging trends of voluntary associations and synagogues as models for their own life together.

In *Re-Imagining Life Together in America* we have proposed that this community-centered character of early Christian literature can help con-temporary churches in their address to the American disaster of pervasive individualism through the enlivenment of church community. Although not simple, this help from early Christian communities is possible. Looking to these early Christian communities for help as a part of an American search for community today would involve the following:

> Early Christianity, even in its New Testament forms, cannot function straightforwardly as models. The way these traditions are received by our day must be nuanced with an appreciation of the relative historical perspectives that time and our time exhibit. In addition, the differences both among various early Christian groups and among particular cultural settings today dare not be overlooked. Inasmuch as some modeling from early Christianity for twenty-first century America can occur, delicate attention must be paid to which particular early Christian com-munity can serve as an example for which particular cultural set-ting in America today. So, the two edges of such learning must be observed. First of all, the hope that there is one model from early Christianity for our day must be abandoned. Neither the diversity of early Christian communities nor the many interest-ing differences among Christian groups today merit reducing search for community to one model. Secondly, the valid hope for some models from early Christian communities for some particu-lar situations today must be honored. In fact, it is the multiplic-ity of community models from early Christianity that provides powerful impetus to the possibility of new and energized Christian communities today. Early Christian diversity actually

How much about the world did early Christians ignore or just be uninformed of because their communities were too small?

encourages us to appropriate these traditions by examining the ways particular models from the past may inform and inspire specific communities today. (21)

The Historical Jesus and Community Formation

Against this background I want to assess how much the historical Jesus as we have painted him during our last seventeen years of Jesus Seminar scholarship can help in the crucial work today of bringing Americans together into community. I do this, not because such community-building work is the only meaning the historical Jesus might take on for us and our contemporaries,[5] but because it is a way of coming to terms with the particular American circumstances as outlined above.

The historical Jesus himself in community. Our work in the Jesus Seminar seems ambiguous on the question of how much the historical Jesus himself participated in community. We have on the one hand rejected the historicity of the traditions of "the Twelve" and "the apostles" as historical groups convened by Jesus. We have also tended to view the historical Jesus within the models of aphorist and sage, and have emphasized the iconoclastic and unique characters of his teachings. We have not placed his healings within a community of healers as do Hebrew scriptures for the healing traditions of Elijah and Elisha. On the early hand, one of our more thoroughly published Seminar members, John Dominic Crossan, has clearly articulated a strategy of "commensality" by the historical Jesus,[6] although this notion has not necessarily become a part of the Seminar's database.

Consultation with our actual voting on the deeds of Jesus indicates no red or pink votes for actions of Jesus that bring people together. For instance, such convening actions in the gospels as the feeding of the five thousand, the calling of the disciples, the last supper of Jesus, or the gathering in the synagogue according to Luke 4 did not receive red or pink votes.

A similar conclusion results from examination of the voting on Jesus' sayings. None of the red or pink sayings portray Jesus as calling people together or urging people to build ways of being in community. Only in Luke 9:59 and its parallel, Matthew 8:22, did Jesus' words, "Follow me" receive a pink vote. Even there *The Five Gospels* is quick to add: "It is conceivable that 'Follow Me!' arose as an isolated injunction of Jesus. If so, it was probably coined in connection with a saying like the one recorded in Luke 9:59: Jesus says 'Follow Me!' to someone who first wants to go and bury his father." (46) In other words, it is not at all clear that Jesus is understood as convening a group around him. The words "Follow me!"

may be more a contrast between the lifestyle of Jesus and following family burial traditions.

Similarly the Jesus Seminar's votes concerning the instructions to the "twelve" or "seventy-two" about what to do while on the road were generally voted black and gray. The only two instructions receiving pink votes were those instructing followers after entering one town to stay in one house and accept the food offered to them (Luke 10:7, 8; Thom 14:4). *The Five Gospels* comments: "the Fellows concluded that the instructions were older than their incorporation into written gospels, but they were sharply divided on whether any of them could be traced directly back to Jesus." (63) This provides then scant evidence or conviction that the historical Jesus was either part of a community or tried to found a community of followers.[7] The historical Jesus is pictured in the votes of the Jesus Seminar as a "laconic sage"[8] with some followers, rather than a convener or founder of a community.

Four caveats, however, to this initial conclusion about Jesus' teachings must be noted: 1) The very act of teaching brought people together. What we know about teaching itself in first-century Galilee indicates that it was done in and depended on communal settings of meals and marketplace. 2) The teachings themselves also refer to communal institutions such as meals, marketplace, family, and village. 3) The teachings about the "reign of God" certainly imply a social dimension. Although the historical Jesus' teachings about the "reign of God" do not seem to reference a specific group, it does assume a larger, if somewhat amorphous, collectivity. 4) It is assumed by most scholars that the historical Jesus saw himself as a part of the people of Israel, a social and mythical category.

It is then appropriate to conclude that Jesus' consciousness was deeply social and assumed a belonging to larger social bodies. This larger social belonging, however, does not seem to indicate allegiance to or interest in specific group or community membership. In this regard then we note that the portraits of the historical Jesus coming from the Jesus Seminar do not provide much direct subject matter about community, its importance, or the dynamics of forming community. This stands in marked contrast to the portraits of Jesus in the gospels, apocalypses, instruction manuals, and letters of early Christianity, where the more mythologized Jesus shows great interest in a wide array of community dynamics.

It is interesting to note that this conclusion about the historical Jesus and community building is actively interpreted in different ways today. In contrast to the values promoted in this essay, many (especially individualist or church-alienated) interpreters find great comfort in the historical Jesus' distance from the task of community building. Given the

Why people reject christian community?

enormous mistakes and massive violence done to individuals during the history of Christianity in exact reference to adherence to community, such current day embrace of the historical Jesus' avoidance of community themes needs to be appreciated as well.

Texts and community formation in America

Just because it appears the historical Jesus did not strongly promote community does not mean that contemporary historical Jesus portraits cannot assist in the vital task of teaching Americans how to live together more closely. This is especially true given the way any texts function to convene and nurture community in western religions and to some extent in non-western religions.

Reading texts together in Islam, Judaism, and Christianity is a deeply "inculturated" way of convening, deepening, and nuancing community throughout the West. The larger Midrashic project of Judaism in which community discussion of texts is the occasion for the production of more texts, which are then the occasion for more community discussion and more texts is perhaps the best example of how western religions of the book depend on texts in their community formation. But both Islam and Christianity are also replete with practices of communal reading, rereading, and misreading in order to bring people together, to help understand life together, to establish ways of living together, and to change existing ways of living together.

CREATING UNDER-STANDING

In this regard it seems inevitable that a corpus of texts in the West such as the pink and red sayings of the historical Jesus have power to convene, shape, reform, and renew community. As such, this conference itself provides strong and helpful evidence of the historical Jesus' community building promise in our day. This conference indeed marks an important moment in the conjunction of historical Jesus discourse and community building in America in its convening of actual community leaders around historical Jesus themes.

What is both magical and ironic about this process in which we are now engaged is that it is inevitably mythologizing. That is, our efforts to bring the historical Jesus into dialogue with our particular historical and community dynamics in the twenty-first century require an imagination that springs us beyond first-century Galilee and into an imaginal, meaning-making sphere. As we begin to name Jesus as a "stand-up comic" or "advocate for women's rights" or "artist," we enter the imaginal and mythologizing process that so many other readers of the material in other ages have. This process allows us to affirm meaning, and perhaps community, for our time, but it loosens our connection to the role of the historian, who attempts to remain true to an ancient optic.

leavening up shaking up

The historical Jesus corpus and specific community building tasks today

Since the founding of the Jesus Seminar in 1985, I have been both an academic and a pastor. Almost all of my work as a professor has been at the graduate level. All of my work as a pastor has been in church renewal settings, in which I have been a part of changing a dying congregation into a growing one. In both settings I have actively promoted and engaged historical Jesus work. This has also resulted in extensive interactions with various church groups nationally through my own speaking engagements. In this section of this essay I want to assess how much or little the historical Jesus has helped in various dimensions of my pastoral experience of community building.

Adult education

Over the past seventeen years in my congregations and for those to whom I have spoken around the country, adult educational programming has been one of the liveliest arenas for engagement of the historical Jesus. The process of studying and discussing anything within a church nurtures its community. Studying the historical Jesus has seemed most helpful to a certain segment of churchgoers. This segment has been those over the age of forty-five who have had substantial Christian upbringing. Study about the historical Jesus has helped free this segment of people from past presumptions and dogmatics in their church upbringing, and has therefore bonded these people to one another in the processing of this new critical perspective on Jesus. Very little interest in the historical Jesus has been evident in those under the age of thirty-five. This segment of churchgoers—often much less familiar with any Christian material—remains skeptical of scholarly representations and deeply desirous to reclaim some historical traditions of spirituality on a variety of terms.

Children's formation and belonging

Here also a distinction needs to be made according to age. Small children, including those through the first several grades of schooling, do not seem interested in or critically able to engage distinctions between story and historicity. Any stories help these children feel a part of the community in which the stories are told. Some stories from the Bible seem especially attractive to these children, while other Bible stories seem especially puzzling and off-putting. It is not, however, the less historically accurate and more imaginative stories that are problematic. Rather, stories with subject matter that is beyond their developmental capacity (e.g., extreme violence, sexuality, and cultural differences) are the less interesting for them. On the other hand, as children develop critical capacities, their interest in historical Jesus questions increases. Over the last seventeen years I have seen this developmental stage lower its threshold from the ages of twelve to thirteen to ten to eleven.

Worship

Worship is by far the strongest community building experience in the congregations I have served. (preaching is here somewhat artificially excluded from this worship category and will be considered as a separate category.) My congregations' experiences of a wide variety of people speaking personal joys, concerns, and prayers; singing eclectic music; watching and participating in dance and drama; participating in communion; and contributing to a variety of rituals using rocks, flowers, candles, and art has been central to their growing allegiance to one another. In my speaking engagements around the country this is also true of a growing number of new or renewed church settings,[9] but not so true of other more conventional churches. The historical Jesus has played hardly any role in this dimension of church community building by virtue of two factors: 1) our Jesus Seminar portrait of him does not show him at all in worship settings of his own time, and therefore it is more difficult to link contemporary worship expression to him; and 2) the iconoclastic nature of many of the historical Jesus texts requires a more thoughtful and less symbolic engagement characteristic of worship.

Forming inclusive community and integrating marginalized groups into church community

My congregations have become radically inclusive. As each congregation grew, inclusion of various racial groups, various classes, women, queer, and otherly-abled persons became a substantial hallmark of the communities. Study and preaching about the historical Jesus, especially in his own boundary-crossing efforts, nurtured this part of our community building in substantial ways. The category-breaking character of the parables, the humorous and critical nature of the aphorisms, and the meal associations with marginalized persons within the historical Jesus corpus has regularly been helpful both for our own marginalized people and for those more mainstream persons growing into a more inclusive understanding of community. Of course, this is also true of a number of other parts of other Christian literature besides the historical Jesus material.

Pastoral counseling

Pastoral counseling often serves crucial roles in community building. Especially for the majority of my congregants who have not had much experience in churches, the availability of a pastor to think through occasional personal issues comes as a welcome surprise to those in a highly individualized, secular society. Inasmuch as ancient material is occasionally useful in pastoral counseling settings, historical Jesus material seems helpful with persons trying to imagine new possibilities for their lives. The other main type of pastoral counseling—dealing with people in pain and distress—does not seem to be helped by references to the historical Jesus.

Reaching out to situations of social, economic, and ecological need

Church (or other) communities are much stronger, when they go beyond their own situations and experience solidarity with situations of social, economic, or ecological need. Breaking churches out of sectarian and self-referential frames allows their community to be more supple and energized. In this community-enhancing task, historical Jesus material has occasionally helped to break church people out of old patterns. However, the paucity of historical Jesus material that shows him directly engaged in situations of social or economic need makes the material only marginally useful. Similarly, the lack of any texts showing Jesus organizing a group of people to address a situation of need is inhibitive. Non-historical Jesus material from the gospels of Matthew and Luke are much more helpful in assisting churchgoers to address directly situations of human need. Relative to situations of ecological need, the historical Jesus' use of a number of natural metaphors for the "reign of God" has been helpful in affirming church connection to the earth.

Spiritual growth

Development of spiritual practice and discipline, as noted above, is a special interest of both many church-alienated adults and a great many baby-busters and generation X members. Inasmuch as churches can provide imaginative takes on traditional Christian spirituality, these persons become deeply bonded to church community. My book, *Jesus Before God: The Prayer Life of the Historical Jesus* came out of my bi-vocational experience of being a member of the Jesus Seminar and a pastor. The last third of that book proposes ways of applying the unconventional prayer life of the historical Jesus to contemporary spiritual practice. It also acknowledges my larger experience that spiritual seekers are interested in many other spiritual practices—both Christian and non-Christian.

Helping people to become acquainted and to work together

One of the main tasks in church community building is encouraging people to become acquainted. A second, related task is helping diverse people work together in community tasks. The lack of settings in which the historical Jesus was engaged in either of these tasks makes it less frequent that he becomes a model for these community-building tasks. By and large, material from the later gospels and letters seem to take these tasks more seriously. When either working together or becoming acquainted is blocked by prejudice or hesitancy to engage difference, reference to the historical Jesus has occasionally been helpful.

Preaching

My experience in building local church community assumes that preaching integrates all of the above categories of church life. I and my co-pastors try to present sermons that address personal crises, socioeconomic factors, ecological issues, the need for adult and children's education, the challenge of becoming inclusive in community, the challenge of working together, the need to learn spiritual practice, and the importance of symbolic, worshipful activity. Following the lectionary by and large, we engage one particular text each Sunday as it intersects with dimensions of our community life. Our general experience is that the congregation(s) respond(s) excitedly to preaching that is both intellectually rigorous and emotionally expressive. Although in my earlier ministry I was wary of Protestantism's fixation on preaching, I am now convinced that integrative and expressive preaching is vital to the building of church community.

My preaching colleague(s) is/are generally, of course, not as versed in historical Jesus material as I am. I regularly address issues of historicity in the sermon. Sometimes as an aside I indicate that, for instance, a Johannine text on which I am preaching is not historically reliable. Other times, when the lectionary includes a text with red or pink material in it, I focus on the historical Jesus' message. Still other times, in a text with both red/pink and gray/black material I choose to focus on the non-historical Jesus portion of the text because it connects more directly to current issues of the congregation's lives. Overall, I have found that the historical Jesus material is helpful in this preaching rhythm. Congregants are sometimes pleasantly surprised and often reassured by my willingness to address issues of historicity. The particular value of the historical Jesus for preaching corresponds almost exactly to the above, overall assessment of the historical Jesus for church community building. When preaching about inclusiveness, issues for people over forty-five, and issues of imagining life differently, the historical Jesus is regularly useful. When preaching about working together, reaching out to people in need, spiritual practice, and personal pain, invoking the historical Jesus is less useful than many other early Christian texts. Or conversely, preaching on an historical Jesus text tends to address issues about inclusiveness, issues for people over forty-five, and issues of imagining life differently, whereas preaching on another kind of text has advantages in addressing the other issues.

Conclusion

In addressing the larger task of community building in America through local churches, the historical Jesus helps to some degree. Being able to distinguish the historical Jesus from other layers of Christian tradition is quite helpful in the ways it both identifies him as a particular expression and model and in ways that it frees (mostly older Christians) from doctrinal and other traditional presumptions. Serious community building in America through churches needs the historical Jesus, historical Jesus scholarship, other early Christian models and expressions, other contemporary innovations and expressions, other non-Christian spiritual traditions, patient and imaginative leadership skills, the presence of population groups outside the churches, and constant self-critique.

The Jesus Seminar in Africa

Glenna S. Jackson

"We learned to love you and we trusted you—and then you
gave us these books." (Samuel Dzobo, Africa University,
September 2000)

Six weeks later:

"Prof, I don't know how you could vote red on that story.
There's no way Jesus could have said that!" (Tafadzwa Mabambe)

Preface

~~Boytes~~

I teach Jesus Seminar materials in four different venues: to undergraduates at Otterbein College in Westerville, Ohio; to undergraduates and
graduates at Africa University in Mutare, Zimbabwe; to course-of-study
students with a variety of educational backgrounds at Methodist
Theological School of Ohio; and to an adult study class consisting of
laypersons and retired pastors at Church of the Messiah United Methodist
in Westerville, Ohio. If I were to state a thesis at this point of my involvement with these four venues, it would be this: In traditional settings in
the Western world, the Jesus Seminar provides freedom for intellectual
survival in the church with the potential for systemic change. In contrast,
the Jesus Seminar provides inspiration for third-world people to make
immediate systemic change. This essay is based on my experience in an
African context.[1]

Introduction

As a newcomer to the Continent of Africa nearly three years ago, I was immediately humbled as a New Testament scholar because I discovered quickly that Africans (the students in this particular class were from Zimbabwe, Mozambique, Burundi, and Angola) know far more and have better insights into the study of the New Testament than we as westerners could ever possibly hope to have. One of the classes I taught at Africa University during the fall semester of 2000 was to fourth-year students (seniors), who graduated that next June with bachelor of divinity degrees; the title of the class was "The Parables of Jesus." The first time I went to Zimbabwe I raised over US $4,000 to buy textbooks and library books. The books I chose for this particular course were *Remedial Christianity*, *The Five Gospels*, and *The Acts of Jesus*. (And life could have been so easy!) As luck would have it, and even though the books arrived before I did, we were unable to get the books out of customs until the fifth week of class. But I am lucky: all I really need is a Bible to teach. It was a glorious day when the books arrived in the classroom. These students had never owned new books and so they took these three with eager anticipation. In fact, they stayed up all night as a group to read. When I arrived in class the next morning, I was greeted with absolute silence. I began the class with a typical Shona greeting and received absolute silence. I asked a question and again received absolute silence. In desperation, I sat down and said, "None of us is leaving this classroom until someone tells me what's going on." As they looked at each other uncomfortably in what seemed to be an interminable amount of time, Samuel Dzobo finally stood up and said, "Prof, we learned to love you and we trusted you. (Silence.) And then you gave us these books." He sat down. Silence. I picked my heart up off the floor, reminded myself that life could have been easy, found my voice, and said, "Okay, we've got work to do. Get out your books." As the weeks progressed, the students began to say things like, "I can't believe you voted red on this story; there's no way Jesus could have said that. . . . Pink isn't the right color for that saying, black is." On the last day of class, Dzobo once again stood up to address me: "Prof, we understand and we even like the historical Jesus. But, what do we preach on Easter Sunday?" And that is another story.

The Bible in Africa

Contrary to the Western world where books *about* the Bible have now exceeded the sale of Bibles (thus contributing to an ever-growing biblical illiteracy), the Bible itself is probably the most widely read book in Africa. Fidon R. Mwombeki categorizes five different ways that the Bible is used in Africa: 1) the Bible is seen as a symbol of God's presence and protection; e.g., Bibles are placed under pillows, in suitcases, in new houses, and in coffins. 2) The Bible is read for practical utilization, e.g., giving comfort, instruction, exhortation, even condemnation. 3) The Bible does not always have to be understood rationally:

> The biblical reading is appropriated spiritually, emotionally, mystically. The historical setting of a text is not significant, and even less the identity of its author. African spiritualism supersedes intelligibility. Most often, the Bible is appropriated worshipfully, by heart, not necessarily by mind.

4) Some settings do demand intelligibility. Mwombeki's examples include a firstborn seven-year-old boy asking why an angel from God would slaughter the firstborn child of every Egyptian family; defending monogamy in the light of Abraham, David, Solomon, Elkanah, and many others; a young intellectual asking why Africans identify with Israel when they should be identifying with Egyptians, Jebusites, Philistines, and other peoples who were wiped out and driven out of their lands to give way to the migrating Jews. And, 5) there is strong affinity between the religious and cultural context of the Bible and that of contemporary Africa, e.g., people going out to fish for that day's breakfast, beggars and prostitutes in the streets, women carrying the family's load, exclusion of women and children in counts and censuses, light from oil lamps, neighbors going to ask for bread to feed an unexpected guest in the middle of the night, free "all-you-can-eat" weddings for all relatives and friends, demon-possessed men, women, and children, as well as the strong affinity in social arrangements between African and biblical cultures such as lineage, age-grouping, the value of royalty, birthrights and inheritance laws, the value of the elderly, and emotional attachment to ancestral lands.[2]

Critique of Western New Testament Studies

I appreciate critique on western historical-critical studies, including, for example, Kwok Pui-lan's observation that

> New Testament survey books tell us that the first quest for the historical Jesus took place in the nineteenth century. But they do not specify that the quest took place in Europe and there were in fact two quests, not one: the quest for Jesus and the quest for land and people to conquer. Is it mere coincidence that the newest quest for the historical Jesus is taking place in the United States, when the U.S. is trying to create a Pax Americana?[3]

Many current studies include the term "globalization," and I appreciate and even applaud any study that goes beyond a white, male, western viewpoint. At the same time, my limited experience as a first-world white feminist in an African context leads me to agree with many with whom I spoke, i.e., that the term globalization is simply an updated, cleaner-sounding word for colonialization and all that goes with it. In fact, Elder Mukuzwazwa of Old Mutare vehemently argues that "the 'global village' does not exist."

African Stories and Parables

Before I write about the students with whom I had the privilege of meeting at Africa University, I must note Sebastian Bakare's appropriation of the parables in the land crisis that exists in Zimbabwe now. He supports Matthew's sense of God's justice in the parable of the vineyard (Matt 20:1–16) in that the vineyard owner was responding to the needs of the people—everyone needed a day's wage and so it was a day's wage everyone received no matter how long he had worked.[4] In the parable of the tenants (Mark 12:1–12), Bakare claims that [according to Mark] "Jesus succeeds in confronting the ruling class with their own injustice. The retribution which the tenants suffer at the hands of the landlord, and which they readily affirm, will be inflicted on them. As the ruling elite have dispossessed the poor, so they too will be dispossessed."[5] And in the parable of the shrewd manager (Luke 16:1–16), Bakare suggests that the manager identifies himself with the peasants instead of the elite; he no longer fears downward mobility: "His future is now with the peasantry instead of the upper-class. That is what the kingdom of God is like: identifying oneself with the oppressed and exploited peasants and making one's future with them, by fighting for a just socio-economic system."[6] Bakare quotes John Dominic Crossan, "The parable breaks the bond between power and justice. Instead it equates justice and vulnerability."[7]

My students at Africa University also wrote parables and introductions to New Testament parables from their own experiences. Jean Ntahoturi, a Hutu from Burundi, introduced his analysis of the Samaritan (Luke 10:30–35), with this story:

> In 1995, I was shopping in the suburb of Bujumbma when I heard gunfire nearby. Two soldiers were shot dead. The rebels were around. In a confused situation, I ran away in the hills. I was not alone. When we began to climb the hill, one mother realized that her five-year-old son was not with her. She was so disturbed. She decided to go back to look for him. We [tried to] persuade her

not to go back. She refused. "I have to go to look for my son; if I am to die today, there is no option," she said. When she was moving around, the child saw his mother very far. He was in rebels' hands. He started crying. The rebels suddenly saw the mother and called her to come and take the child. First, she was afraid, but she got courage and she approached them and took the child.

And so, according to Jean, one should identify with the victim rather than with the so-called Good Samaritan because help comes from the most unexpected source, in this case, a soldier from the enemy tribe.

In the Parable of the Barren Tree (Luke 13:6–9), Jean wrote the following as an introduction:

The Kudzunga family rejoiced when their elder son got married. Everyone in the family looked forward to the success of this couple (Tatenda and Tendai). After the wedding day the aunts expected their sister-in-law to have conceived. Two months, five months, a year, there were no signs of pregnancy. One of the aunts was bold enough, she went and asked her brother, Tatenda. She said, "Tatenda, what is going on between you and Tendai? It is high time that you should have a child." Tatenda calmly responded, "Auntie, give us one more chance; we will do it, just allow us to look into the issue." The auntie finally said, "If your wife is barren you better divorce her and marry somebody who is productive or you better marry a second wife who will give you children."

Jean not only understood the story of the barren fig tree perfectly, but he also comprehended the consequences of barrenness in a more enlightened and critical manner than my own understanding.

As we were talking about the Parables of the Hidden Treasure (Matt 13:44//Thom 109:1–3) and the Pearl (Matt 13:45–46//Thom 7:1–2), Sophirina Sign, an associate pastor at Old Mutare Mission and student in the parables class, said that she understood the stories exactly because her uncle had been trying to get her elderly grandmother to leave her tiny plot of land and to live with him. But the grandmother refused to leave because a long time ago she had buried a treasure; she couldn't remember where she buried it or what even the treasure was, but she certainly wasn't going to leave it.

A typical, and recent, exegetical commentary on the Parable of the Hidden Treasure goes as follows:

The hiding of valuables in the earth is an age-old method of storing them safely. According to Josephus, in the aftermath of their conquest of Jerusalem (A.D. 70), the Romans discovered gold, silver, and other treasured articles that had been stored underground "in view of the uncertain fortunes of war," and the Copper Scroll from Qumran (3Q15) — which is from the first century A.D. — contains a long list of buried treasures, many items of which are underground. Moreover, in another of Jesus' parables a man is portrayed as hiding money in the ground (Matt 25:18, 25).[8]

My point, of course, is that we don't have to go back two thousand years to gain this understanding, nor do we need to be so incredulous at such practices.

Tafadzwa Mabambe, a Zimbabwean, introduced the Parable of the Wedding Celebration (Matt 22:1–14//Luke 14:16–24//Thom 64:1–12) with these comments:

> In an African context if you are invited to a family occasion, for that moment you are part and parcel of that family. The people who see you will associate you with that family. For this reason one has to make up his or her mind before accepting an invitation; [i.e.,] will you be comfortable to be associated?

As a matter of fact, that notion played out in my flat in Mutare when I invited the class for pizza; before they entered my home — they were literally at the threshold — they let me know that if I invited them in and they came in, then we had a reciprocal notion of family commitment. And Dzobo, also a Zimbabwean, told me that in his village, the entire population gets an invitation to a wedding — i.e., there is no hierarchical or exclusivist guest list. He, therefore, questioned the entire premise of the story that Jesus told: the end of Jesus' parable should have been the normative, not the other way around.

In my final example of this type, that same student, Dzobo, introduced the Parable of the Generous Vineyard Owner (Matt 20:1–15) with this parallel:

> When I was growing up in the village, during the planting season, we used to have some form of cooperative where families in the villages organized themselves to rotate cultivating and planting each family's field. It worked like this: ten families would come together, go to one family's field and plough it and plant the seed. In the afternoon they would go to the next family. In

five days all the fields of the ten families would be ploughed and planted. There were those who would come late to someone's field after working in their own field. Those who came late would argue that "Yatsika yamwa." This is a Shona proverb meaning that even those who do things at the last minute no matter how little effort they have put they are considered to have worked. When those who were late had their turn to have the fields cultivated, people would still go and cultivate. Maybe this is the concept that Jesus was teaching. "Yatsika yamwa" literally meaning a cow that has its feet wet at the river had the chance to drink water.

Application

As you read the next African parable, think about what questions we (westerners) need to ask and have answered to understand the context and meaning of this parable. The explanation by the author will follow.

Parable of the Widow by Samuel Dzobo

It is like the rains have come and everyone is busy in his/her fields. Then a widow has her only two oxen get lost in the forest. For two weeks, she has been looking for the two oxen to no avail. She knows she is late with planting. She goes to her deceased husband's brother to ask him to plough her one field, but he refuses because she refused to be inherited. She goes to another and he refuses because he has not finished ploughing his last field and that his oxen had been tired. The widow then goes to the aunt of her deceased husband to have her son plough her field, but the aunt refuses because her son would want to rest for he had been busy with their own fields. The widow gives up and she knows she cannot plant in her field. Then a friend of her deceased husband comes by and he finds that her field has not been ploughed. He brought his own oxen and ploughs the field and sent his sons to look for the lost oxen. That year the widow had a great harvest, more than anyone else in the village.

What background information or questions about the culture do you need to ask to understand this parable? Some may include: 1) What is "inheritance"? 2) Why are these particular characters included in the story; i.e., what is the role of each? For example, I argue elsewhere that most, if not all, female characters in the gospel stories must be female; since the stories are dependent on their female specificity.[9]

Explanation to Dzobo's Parable of the Widow

In my culture the custom of inheritance is still practised. A woman who refuses to be inherited after the death of her husband is saying, "Leave me alone, I can manage my own life." This woman stays at her home probably because all her daughters are married. The fact that she bore some children makes stay at her home [possible]. Otherwise she would go to her parents if she has no children and refused inheritance. The uncles refused to plough her field because she can do it. For them to plough the field she has to accept inheritance. Her aunt refuses because she is responsible for the inheritance, by refusing the inheritance the widow was disrespecting the aunt. So the widow has no relative in the midst of relatives. Either she accepts inheritance or she has no relative. The other option is that she can go to her parents but she cannot do that because she has children. So the widow is in the midst of nowhere. To lack food would make her depend on the same people whom she refused to be inherited. But her husband had a friend, a "sahwira." This is more than a friend for a friend is "shamwari." A sahwira takes his friend's burdens as his and he can do anything to help a friend like he is doing it to his own family. The friendship is not over because the husband has died. This is what the woman had forgotten that the Sahwira was still there. When he comes along, he helped her in her field and having the lost oxen found and she has a great harvest. The Shona proverb which says *usahwira unokunda ukama* (this Agape kind of relationship cannot be compared to family relationship) subverts conventional wisdom of blood is thicker than water which emphasizes the family relationship as more important than any other relationship. Her uncles were ashamed because of the harvest. (NB The custom of inheritance is fast losing grip because of HIV/AIDS.)

Final Remarks

If you have not already ascertained, part of my agenda is to encourage young African women and men to look at their own cultures for understanding the historical Jesus, the historical evangelists, and historical societies. One of the realizations during the first week of class at Africa University was that, for at least the students working on undergraduate degrees in the faculty of theology, their understanding of early Christianity comes as the result of fundamentalist, white, western missionaries who, in many cases, unloaded a white, male god on them. (God-language is an interesting topic especially when one considers that most students in my classes come from mother tongues that do not use pronouns.) And so for me to enter the scene as a New Testament historian and worse yet, as a fellow in the Jesus Seminar, meant that I was pulling the carpet out from under them—a carpet that had given them hope for a seemingly hopeless situation from which all (not some or many, but all) of them had come and, for that matter, to which all would be returning. By writing and/or retelling their own stories and parables, students began to affirm their own cultures and understanding. In the process, they began to realize that they had something to offer to themselves and to the rest of the world—something that probably surpasses what we think we know from a Western analysis. It is no surprise to most of us that oppression through racism, sexism, and classism was, for the most part, successful because of western greed and was justified by Christianity's patriarchal hierarchy. Mwombeki's two challenges must be included in this discussion: the first is that as a trained reader or theologian, one must

> work through what has been called the 'hermeneutic of reso-
> nance'—to identify the resonance of the biblical text with the
> theology of the church as well as with the situation of the read-
> ers. The situations vary, and each one must be taken seriously
> into account. The second challenge is to face African realities.
> Unless one is in Africa, in the banana groves and the desert
> places, the stinking refugee camps, the crowded town neighbor-
> hoods without proper sanitation, and the hospitals without med-
> icine, one cannot really appreciate how complicated reading the
> Bible is in such situations—and yet, how real.[10]

Incidentally, one of my eight students in the Parables class died of Hepatitis while I was there: a needless death that would not have occurred among my students at Otterbein College in Ohio.

Musa W. Dube adds:

> Unless our critical practice [of biblical studies] takes deliberate
> measures to understand the mechanisms of past and present
> imperialisms—to understand the marriage of imperialism with
> issues of gender, race, class, religion, and sexual orientation—
> even the most liberationist of discourses will end up reinscribing
> the structures of violence and exploitation. . . . Such travels
> should move us from an exclusive focus on one historical period,
> the fortress of the early church, to a concern for the many other

histories of the Christian church; from one religious tradition to the other religious traditions of the world; from an approach that is text-oriented to an approach that makes room for symbols, ritual, art, songs, drama, and poetry. Such travels should also move us not only to read and listen to old stories but also to create new stories, as well as to keep the focus on the aims of our critical practice.[11]

From my limited experience on the Continent of Africa, it appears that Jesus Seminar materials indeed make, and will continue to make, an impact on third-world countries in at least two important ways: 1) people living in African villages exist much like people did in New Testament times and New Testament lands and, therefore, can identify with and clarify for us westerners how life really was; 2) the gist of historical-Jesus sayings mandate a changed world, one where the first shall be last and the last first, one where those who hunger and thirst for justice and those who are poor and hungry are to be congratulated. Even though Nyasha Chimbunde has yet to forgive me for the fact that Mary was not a virgin, he is excited that his life in an impoverished nation has value in the world of historical-Jesus scholarship.

The "Good News" about the Historical Jesus

Charles W. Hedrick

This is not writ in any book.[1]

Prologue

As I write this, I find myself in uncharted waters. I know of no one who has argued that the "historical Jesus" is "good news" for the church,[2] though I know many who think that recovering the historical Jesus[3] is a good thing. On the other hand, I also know many who think that the work of scholars, like the Jesus Seminar, has been a disservice to the church by undermining "faith," and causing doubt. If true, that would not seem to be good news for the church, and I suppose that makes the Jesus Seminar "the Grinch who stole Christmas."

On its surface, the historical importance of recovering Jesus' personal history seems rather self-evident to me. Jesus' personal history is determined by answering the question: What can be known of him through a historical-critical analysis of the earliest Christian texts without recourse to the early Christian kerygma (i.e., what was preached about Jesus)[4] and the later creeds?[5] How else is one to know that myths of kerygma and creed have any sort of grounding in objective history? Put another way: how is one to know if the inferences early Christians drew about Jesus are sanctioned, even if unhistorical?

The study of human history needs no justification, even if the results upset us: it helps us understand who we are and how we got here; hence it helps break the cycle of an eternal present, in which we assume that things have always been the way we think they are. By looking backward we can, if we choose, also project forward, hopefully to claim a more promising future—one that might actually become an improvement over the past. Hence, the study of our past is a way of opening up our future, and ensuring, insofar as possible, that humanity and the church actually do have futures.

If the critical study of our past is a way of claiming our future, every discovery about our past becomes good news—particularly if it causes us to modify views and behaviors in the light of the past; the struggle of the present with the past and future is precisely how the study of history contributes to the future. In that sense, the recovery of the historical Jesus, in spite of the discomfort it now causes the church and professional scholars committed to an "orthodox" faith, is good news. The historical Jesus contributes to the church's future by helping the church understand its origins, and thus helping it to shape its future in the light of its origins.

How We Got Here

The origins of Christianity are not at all clear to historians of Christian origins. So much information is lost in the shadowy past. Only a provocative residue of information about the diverse and vibrant Christian movements active in the first century has survived. We have no Christian artifacts from the first century,[6] and virtually all manuscripts of the New Testament date from the third century and later.[7] Under these conditions, scholars are forced to use much later versions of texts they judge to be written a century or so earlier. The opportunity for deliberate modification of, and accidental change to, the texts seems obvious, particularly in their early period before they came to be regarded as "Holy Writ."[8]

The texts scholars use to study Jesus describe him in remarkably different ways, and these differences complicate knowing precisely what he actually said and did[9]; hence the historian must sift texts and traditions to determine the most plausible history lying behind them. In the twentieth century, an ever-greater number of historians turned their attention to the discrepancies, raising the question: Can the Christ of modern faith survive a rigorous historical analysis of the ancient sources, which present multiple dissonant perspectives of the first-century "human" figure?

Studying Jesus from a historical perspective is a fairly late phenomenon. Since the second century, Jesus was who, and what, the kerygma, the creeds, and the church said he was. Not until the Enlightenment of the eighteenth century did a gap appear between Jesus of Nazareth and the (second-century) Christ of orthodox Christian faith, as represented, more or less, in the traditional creeds of Western Christianity.[10] The gap became a chasm in the twentieth century, and has continued to widen—at least it has for those who study early Christianity from a historical-critical perspective.[11]

At some point, historians will need to examine whether the historical man, Jesus of Nazareth, has common ground with the Christ of faith. The agreements, if any, between these two figures may help us understand how, and perhaps why, Jesus was elevated in the church's faith from Jewish peasant to Messiah to God. My assignment, however, is to evaluate the importance of the historical Jesus for the church.

Premises

1. The early Christian kerygma originated from inferences followers of Jesus drew from his words and deeds. In other words, the personal history of Jesus antedated kerygma. The continuity between kerygma and Jesus' personal history has yet to be argued convincingly—hence the appearance of the gap. Charles H. Dodd reconstructs the early apostolic kerygma known from Paul's letters as follows:

a. "The Prophecies are fulfilled, and the new Age is inaugurated by the coming of Christ.
b. He was born of the seed of David.
c. He died [for our sins] according to the Scriptures, to deliver us out of the present evil age.[12]
d. He was buried.
e. He rose on the third day according to the Scriptures.
f. He is exalted to the right hand of God as Son of God and Lord of the quick and the dead.
g. He will come again as Judge and Saviour of men.[13]

The only information in this kerygma that is historically verifiable is that Jesus was born, died, and was buried. The rest is inference.

In the Acts of the Apostles, on the other hand, Dodd finds three differences between the Jerusalem kerygma of Acts and the kerygma known to Paul:

a. "Jesus is not [in the Jerusalem kerygma of Acts] called 'Son of God.'
b. The Jerusalem kerygma does not assert that Christ died for our sins.
c. The Jerusalem kerygma does not assert that the exalted Christ intercedes for us."[14]

Hence there were different versions of the ancient kerygma, which owe to different inferences made about Jesus.

The earliest extant Christian writings are the letters of Paul (roughly 50–60 CE); and the message of Paul differs remarkably from Dodd's reconstruction of the "Apostolic kerygma." The classic statement of Paul's preaching is provided in his own summary:

> Now I would remind you, brethren, in what terms I preached to you the gospel, which you received, in which you stand, by which you are saved, if you hold it fast—unless you believed in vain. For I delivered to you as of first importance what I also received, that Christ died for our sins in accordance with the scriptures, that he was buried, that he was raised on the third day in accordance with the scriptures, and that he appeared to Cephas, then to the twelve (1 Cor 15:1–5, RSV).

This statement constitutes a "gospel" that antedated Paul (Paul says: "what I also received"); its centerpiece was the preaching of the significance of Jesus' crucifixion (1 Cor 1:17–18, 23–25). Paul understood himself to stand at the significant juncture of two "ages"—a present evil age, which was passing away, and the dawning of a "new" age (1 Cor 10:11). Jesus' death, in some way, brought about this convergence of the aeons. Paul's message derives largely from his understanding of the significance of the death of Jesus. In schematic form, Paul's message has been summarized like this:

1. "Sin has been defeated."
2. "Death has been condemned."
3. "The [deficiency of] the law has been exposed."
4. "Christ has discharged humanity from the curse of the law."
5. Even the creation, which was "subjected to futility. . . will be set free from its bondage to decay" (Rom 8:20–21).
6. "God's sovereignty has been established."
7. Creation presently awaits its judgment.[15]

Paul had very little to say about the historical man, Jesus of Nazareth. His letters preserve only vestiges of Jesus' personal history: he was descended from David, born under the authority of Torah, had a brother (James), ate with his disciples the night before he died, was crucified, and was buried.[16]

Paul shared, without further reflection, the early Christian belief that Jesus was God's Anointed (=Messiah=Christ), who had been promised (Rom 9:5; 15:8–12). God had so designated him when he raised him from death (Rom 1:1–4). Jesus was raised to God's spiritual domain, from whence he would come to claim his own (1 Thess 4:13–18). In the interim, the resurrected Christ also dwells in the consciousness of every believer (Rom 8:9–11).[17] The differences from Dodd's "Apostolic kerygma" are remarkable. The conclusion is inevitable: early Christians drew different inferences about Jesus.

It is striking that these kerygmatic formulae consist for the most part of statements about Jesus' person, and include nothing that he said and did in his public career. In short, what the early church preached about Jesus was not simply a repeat of what Jesus had talked about some twenty years or so earlier; rather, kerygma consisted, in the main, of a series of inferences the early followers of Jesus drew about him and from what was done to him.[18]

The later formal creeds of the Western church are also inferences, but these inferences were drawn from the kerygma and the later faith of the church.[19] The framers of the creeds did not work with a first-hand knowledge of Jesus' personal history; they knew only his kerygmatic history. In response to their clash with non-Christian religions in the first century they drew two further inferences: there was an identity of "substance" between the Father and the Son, and—the second—Father, Son, and Holy Spirit constituted a triune deity. In this regard, it is instructive that both kerygma and, later, creed, virtually ignore the public career of Jesus (what he said and did) in their evaluation of Jesus' significance; they leap from his birth to his death.[20] The Jesus of contemporary orthodox Christian faith, reflected in kerygma and later creed, is an early second-century construct formulated from inferences on early Christian tradition. Its origin cannot be traced any earlier than the second century.

2. The first century, to judge from the few texts that did survive, was characterized by diversity. No one single early Christian kergyma existed in the early period, and even the early Christian tradition from which the kerygma originated was diverse.[21]

3. There can be other inferences. The circumstances of Jesus' personal history were such as to allow different inferences about his public career in the first century. A classic illustration of the problem of the historical Jesus is whether or not Jesus offered a sign, or signs, to validate a commission from God. Mark (8:11–13) says that Jesus refused to give a sign to validate his authority.[22] In a parallel passage in Luke (11:16–32), Jesus offers the sign of Jonah, which Luke interprets as the preaching of Jonah to the city of Nineveh: as Jonah preached to Nineveh and the Ninevites repented, so the Son of Man is preaching to people of his own generation and they are repenting. In another parallel passage in Matthew (12:38–42), Jesus offers the sign of Jonah, which Matthew explains in two

ways: the sign of Jonah is Jonah's preaching to Nineveh, and the resurrection of Jesus—as Jonah was in the great fish for three days and three nights, so the Son of Man is in the earth for that length of time.[23] In the Gospel of John, on the other hand, the public career of Jesus was filled with signs—and none of them is the sign of Jonah.[24] Did Jesus offer a sign to validate his commission, or did he not? Did Jesus offer the sign of Jonah? If he did, did he interpret in only one way—or two ways?

The canonical evangelists drew different inferences from the traditions they had available to them. There is no reason in principle why other inferences may not be drawn from the historical data—even in the twenty-first century. Such inferences are authorized by the diverse inferences made in the first century.

4. The difference between a historian's view of Jesus and Orthodoxy's Jesus rests precisely in the mythic inferences that Orthodoxy drew, and continues to affirm, about Jesus.[25] By definition a historian may not make mythic inferences. Myth describes the activities of gods. Stories describing the activities of the gods are usually set in a time and place different from the world of common experience, but they may also be set in a world recognizable, to some degree, as the mundane world of common human experience.[26] Historians work only at the level of information available to people who do not have a personal stake in the history being described. To be sure, historians can describe what people believe and think about the activities of gods, but the reality they describe when they do is conceived as the social construct of the people holding such views and not as the actual activity of gods. Kerygma and creed, however, were (and are) formed out of "information" available only to people of faith. They are theological constructs, drawing to some extent on historical information, and are conceived as descriptions of actual reality. Certainly, historians, like everyone else, may draw inferences from data, but the data must be as objective as possible, and even the historian's inferences must operate at the level of human cause and effect. In a historian's construct the gods are not players. Orthodoxy's Jesus is mythicized; the historian's Jesus cannot be mythicized. That is to say, inference must never be confused with data.

5. Properly speaking, the "historical Jesus" is not a construct, but a disassociated collection of raw data, brought together in no particular order on the basis of the most rigorous historical criteria—a hodgepodge of information and not Jesus as he actually was. Ideally the criteria are designed to identify information that would have been accessible to the most neutral witness to Jesus' public career. Thus, the criteria exclude, or should exclude, all early Christian inferences about Jesus drawn from the

data. A historical description of Jesus' personal history, by definition, must exclude every inference drawn by the early Christian communities. A historical vita may include only data that could have been verified in the first century by a disinterested party to the events.

Modern historians obviously are not eyewitnesses to Jesus' public career. They must work with texts written, at the earliest, a generation or more after Jesus' death. The authors of these texts were not themselves eyewitnesses, nor apparently did they use eyewitness resources.[27] They used oral reports about Jesus, which circulated among early church communities after his death.[28] This tradition about Jesus was remarkably diverse. While it did contain some historical information, it also contained legends, inferences, myths, misinformation, Christian theology and belief, sayings of early Christian prophets, and things that had nothing to do with the historical man at all.[29] Modern historians have developed rigorous criteria for sorting through the multilayered traditions reflected in the gospels; the criteria exclude *possible* historical information in favor of what *most probably* originates with the historical man.[30] The most probable information is the raw data recovered by the Jesus Seminar; it constitutes a residue of Jesus' personal history.

Modern historians, like the framers of kerygma and creed, may also draw inferences from the data and develop a construct, or a profile, of Jesus from the data, as members of the Jesus seminar have done using their two reports: *The Five Gospels*[31] and *The Acts of Jesus*.[32] The recently published book *Profiles of Jesus*[33] is a series of different profiles of Jesus, sketched by fourteen members of the Jesus Seminar, in which each draws on aspects of Jesus' personal history identified by the Seminar. To organize data into profile, inferences must be made about the data; thus profiles are not to be confused with the historical data itself.

The Good News about the Historical Jesus

By "good news" I do not mean to imply that historical information about Jesus should be conceived as some kind of "gospel." As I said above, I understand "the historical Jesus" as a collection of disassociated bits of the most probable historical information about Jesus' personal history. The raw data exclude inferences, and constitute the residue of Jesus' personal history—everything that remains of the historical man that a disinterested historical methodology can validate with a high degree of probability.[34] Profiles of Jesus developed out of these historical traditions are also not "gospels," since profiles simply arrange the disassociated information in a kind of vita of the man. A "gospel of the historical Jesus" would necessarily involve both inferences drawn from the data and some kind of advocacy for human behavior, such as we find in the early Christian gospels. The residue of Jesus' personal history is simply "matter-of-fact" information. It has the potential to become "gospel," however, if and when someone argues the contemporary ethical significance of the data for human life—like the church now proclaims for the Christ of Orthodox faith. Such advocacy has generally not been the scholar's role, except in the case of those scholars who see themselves as servants of the church. Advocacy for Jesus has traditionally been the church's role.

There are, at least, two reasons why the "historical Jesus" is good news for the church—there may be others.

1. The "historical Jesus" (the raw historical data) offers the church an opportunity—not available since the first century—to recreate itself and its gospel for the twenty-first century. For nearly 2000 years Jesus of Nazareth has been represented to the world in terms of later inferences drawn from his sayings and deeds rather than in terms of what he himself did and said. This second-century orthodox construct completely obscures the tunic of Jesus' own "homespun" personal history, by shrouding it in the heavy brocaded robe of myth. The peasant has become so exalted that the human is all but swallowed up in divinity. The question is: Does the church follow Jesus, or Jesus as kerygma and creed construe him?

The second-century orthodox representation of Jesus is not historical. In fact, it does not even agree with any one of the first-century gospel interpretations, which already had mythicized him—although they describe him in a way much closer to his peasant roots than do kerygma and creed. In a real sense, the early Christian gospels are more "historical" than kerygma and creed. They, at least, have provided some historical information about what Jesus did and said, while kerygma and creed ignore the historical man and his message, construing him only in terms of their own inferences. What was important in kerygma and creed was not who he was, but who he was in the faith of the church—not what he said and did, but what the church believed about him. At the end of this process Mary's child became God. That being the case, why would anyone then care about the mundane details of his public career?

Recovering even a residue of Jesus' personal history liberates the first-century peasant, and challenges the church to reevaluate itself—and its constructs of faith in the light of Jesus' ideas and career—to face its past and consider its future. The freedom to be yourself is a good thing; so I think Jesus would regard the liberation of his personal history from kerygma and creed a "good thing"[35]—and so will the church, if it is interested in Jesus.

2. The "historical Jesus" offers the church in the twenty-first century an opportunity to draw its own inferences about Jesus. The only other time in history that this was possible was in the first century. At that time, the general view of reality was mythic, and explanations of natural phenomena were generally mythical.[36] But since the Enlightenment of the eighteenth century, a modern scientific view of reality has increasingly made inroads into Western culture. Generally we do not explain mental illness and disease by demon possession; dead people don't come back to life;[37] virgins don't have babies; pigs may be trained and are exceptionally smart, but they don't talk; and people don't walk on water—except metaphorically.

In the first-century world, significance and importance were assessed mythically. For example, ascribing divinity to a human being was a way of paying homage to an exceptional life. Augustus declared Julius Caesar divine, saying that the genius (spirit) of the emperor deserved to be worshiped; temples were erected in Julius Caesar's honor and sacrifices made in his name. He was not the only emperor, or individual, in Graeco-Roman antiquity to be so divinized, however; there were many other sons of god in Graeco-Roman antiquity with whom Jesus competed.

True, human beings have mythy minds, and live by myths (not all religious) devised by their own restless and fertile imaginations. Nevertheless, in the twenty-first century in Western culture, people generally do not think mythically—at least not at the level of their practical living. When sick, they consult a physician rather than a faith healer; when someone hears voices, they are referred to a psychiatrist rather than an exorcist; people think of the earth as neither flat nor the center of the universe, but as spherical and situated in an insignificant corner of the universe; the world is not "peopled" with good spirits and bad, demons and angels; "evil powers" are not supernatural but terrorist nations; and in normal discourse "divine" is how our wives (or husbands) look, and it simply means "exceptionally marvelous." Hence a religious message cloaked in an archaic and outworn mythology will increasingly become a hard sell in rational Western culture in the twenty-first century. The church took about 100 years to transform pagan culture into the Holy Roman Empire.[38] But the relatively short period from 313 CE (Constantine's endorsement of Christianity) to about 440 CE (after which date no pagan is included among Rome's elite) was possible only because of the political marriage between the church and the Roman state at the beginning of the fourth century, as is made clear by Christianity's relatively slow progress in its first 300 years.[39] Even though it was politically disfranchised, however, paganism continued to flourish into the fifth and sixth centuries.[40] In other words, the worldview of paganism died slowly, or was residually and gradually assimilated into Christianity. A similar shift from an ancient mythology to a scientific worldview under the influence of rationalism has been underway since the Enlightenment (eighteenth century), but without enjoying the political advantage Christianity had in the fourth century and later.

In the last century, New Testament mythology was formally recognized in the writings of scholars within the church as a serious problem affecting the church's relevance in the modern world.[41] In the twenty-first century, the archaic worldview, which swallowed Jesus' personal history in the first century, will eventually seriously frustrate and cripple the church's evangelistic efforts. Through the entire history of the church, leaders have had to devise techniques to avoid a blatant clash between modern science and the Bible, which might lead to the recognition that the king's "old suit of clothes" is threadbare. For example, instead of facing head-on obvious difficulties in a biblical passage, a minister or teacher will obliquely ask, "What spiritual lessons do we get from this text?"—as if biblical narratives were written for divining "spiritual lessons," which ignore the obvious.

Many church folk make an exception for what they were taught in their youth, and, by a willing suspension of disbelief for a few hours each week, they are able to continue their long association with the church. But what happens when such people decide they can no longer live with the inconsistency of suspended disbelief and conclude that faith may simply not require them to believe something they know to be patently false? The twenty-first-century question for the church will be: How long can it count on suspended disbelief to shore up the outworn myths of its mythical gospel?

In the last few years we have experienced a resurgence of conservatism and traditionalism in America. Nonetheless, the handwriting is on the wall—in the West we live in a basically rationalistic society in which first-century myths are no longer viable. The ancient view of reality has been steadily falling into obsolescence since the Enlightenment, albeit somewhat more slowly than the ancient gods did. The mysterious voice that announced the death of the Great God Pan in the first century was, in the final analysis, correct, although the worship of Pan continued for several centuries after the announcement.[42] Today Pan's groves and worship centers are silent, just as the earth is not the center of the universe and no longer flat.[43] A "sign of the times" is how clashes between science and the Bible are handled. In my own denomination (Southern Baptist) Sunday School publications address the disjunctions by selectively avoiding difficult Bible passages and subtly reinforcing a first-century mythology where possible. By avoiding the questions, they hope the problems will disappear.

Church Evangelism in the twenty-first century will eventually have to deal with the question: Must potential converts swallow a first-century view of reality to become part of the faith community? Thinking people, who were not nourished at the bosom of mother church during their childhoods, will have the most problem with first-century mythology, and in the long term they will not be alone. If the church answers the question in the affirmative (i.e., being Christian means I must accept a first-century view of reality), the church will eventually find an outworn mythology is a serious obstacle to twenty-first-century faith. A second question is equally important: If I do not have to accept first-century mythology as a part of my faith, what then is the nature of the faith I am invited to share? Put another way: What is the nature of a demythologized, or remythologized, faith in the twenty-first century?

The good news is that the historical Jesus brings us closer to the origin of the early Christian movements—as close as we are ever likely to get. The historical Jesus, freed of the mythical inferences his followers drew in the first century and later, facilitates a historical encounter not possible since the first century. Faced with the historical Jesus, a modern seeker begins largely on the same footing as Jesus' earliest followers. Faced with the historical Jesus, the church has the option of holding to kerygma and creed, or reevaluating the data, drawing what inferences seem appropriate for a different culture and time. Reevaluation of the data is the church's first step to developing a new idiom and rhetoric for the twenty-first century.

Reevaluating Jesus is not a novel idea. The first-century church did it to develop its kerygma, and the later church did it to develop the creeds. There is precedent. When early Christians were confronted with the secularity of Jesus' parables, they made them more religious by the interpretations they appended to them. They inferred that Jesus, being who he was in their faith, must have been saying more in the secular stories than met the eye, and they simply reevaluated the parables in terms of their changed situation.

The first great crisis of faith was the death of Jesus: how could God allow his messiah to die? Jesus' followers solved it by arguing Jesus' death was not accidental, but it always was a part of God's plan (Acts 2:23).

Thus the cross eventually became Orthodoxy's symbol for Christian faith. But not all early Christians dealt with Jesus' death that way. The author of the Gospel of Thomas, for example, made nothing of the death of Jesus. What is important in Thomas is what Jesus said, and not what was done to him. His words brought life, not his death.

Caveat Lector

Let the reader beware! The historical Jesus (just the raw data of his personal history) does not seem a very practical basis on which to found a religious community. Perhaps, it could provide the basis for certain ethical behaviors, but a religious community requires "something more." My students constantly chide me about deleting all the "mystery" from faith. Mystery, the inexplicable or the unordinary, is something, apparently, that human beings need in their religious communities—at least some early Christians found it necessary for their faith.[44] For that reason, the simple residue of Jesus' personal history will very likely not have a broad-based appeal to modern religious communities. In short, the "historical Jesus" will not "preach"—although he may be effective in mitigating the most egregious aspects of Orthodoxy's Jesus.

The raw data of Jesus' personal history is a hodgepodge, but Jesus was a whole human being. Thus, the historical data must be reassembled into profiles providing a tentative reconstructed whole from the parts, such as Robert Funk has done in his *A Credible Jesus*.[45] The profiles are necessary for balance—to insure insofar as possible that no one feature among the fragments may be unfairly exploited to the neglect of the whole. Selecting individual historical fragments as a basis for preaching and neglecting the whole is precisely the "historical heresy" that led to the Orthodox Jesus. Profiles are always tentative sketches of what the whole may have been. They do not present Jesus as he actually was; they help us see how he may have appeared to a neutral eye.

Inferences are drawn from the whole to form the basis for a new idiom and a new rhetoric for the church. First-century preaching about Jesus was successful because it provided the church with an idiom and rhetoric fitting its culture, and because it described how Jesus was significant in that culture. The same must be done for the historical Jesus in the twenty-first century. This is the church's responsibility, which it may decline to accept, but only at the peril of its continued existence.

Even Jesus' early followers did not find the historical man all that appropriate for their message, and they contextualized him in kerygma and creed—in short, they needed "mystery." And little wonder—the ethics of the historical man are more than daunting.[46] His indirect provocative parables do not lend themselves to catechisms. He did not endorse conventional morality, but criticized it, and the residue of his personal history is just as likely to rub against twenty-first century morality. He didn't make many establishment friends, but rather censured the wealthy. He seemed to think that accumulating wealth and serving God were mutually exclusive, but in our world we know that we need the material to further the cause of the spiritual. He advocated nonresistance of evil and actual love of enemies—neither of which seems very practical on a modern global scale. His soul mates were the outsiders—the poor and irreverent, but the church, as it exists today, is the establishment—reverent, well off, and patriotic. Since he was a first-century human being, Jesus shared the mythical worldview of the first century to some degree. He apparently believed in demons, the mana of God's Imperial Rule, and Satan's control of the world. His idea that Satan's evil empire was falling and God's Imperial Rule was winning seems falsified by his death. While this or that aspect of the historical man may be relevant in the modern world, if taken in moderation, the whole is not likely to play well in middle-class churches in the heartland of America.

> *Nevertheless, the historical Jesus is the tiny mustard seed, which, planted in the human heart, produced a gospel that literally changed the world.*

He awaits the church's response. His challenging ethics and strong faith may form the basis of a new vitality for the twenty-first century church; his deep concern for the poor, sick, and outsider may provide the church with a new focus; his personal faith in God may generate new "mysteries" for faith; his parables in which people experienced God in their own ways may suggest a new kind of evangelism; his message about the Imperial Rule of God could generate powerful new symbols for the twenty-first century, and his ideas may be seminal for a new idiom. The way forward is by going backward to the residue of the personal history of Jesus, reassessing it, re-envisioning it, drawing new inferences from the data—in short, developing a gospel for the twenty-first century.[47]

In a sense, the church is in the same situation today as Judaism was in the first century: what to do with the first-century Jew, Jesus of Nazareth? In the first century, mythicizing the man eclipsed his personal history, leading to kerygma and creed and a christianizing of the West. It remains to be seen whether the historical man can provide a similar catalyst for the church in the twenty-first century.

Preaching the New Faith

Francis Macnab

We face a huge task. It is so diffuse it defies specific definition. We all know the task is there: to persuade people and cultures of the world that the 'God' they say they believe in has outgrown 'his' need for body bags and human blood.*

The task is to persuade people and cultures of the world that religion is essentially a binding-together not a tearing-apart. The task is to persuade people and cultures to embrace a new nature of a generous and compassionate heart, of human rights that are real as God's acceptance of us all, of the preservation and celebration of life on Planet Earth.

The task is huge, and God is the problem. God does not come striding over the majestic Afghan mountains with the tidings of peace. God does not bind up the brokenhearted, locked-up, rejected refugees. God does not release people held without an advocate in prisons around the world, nor those in prison to their own prejudice and hate, their politics of fear and greed.

Flowing through, under and around the people of the world are the toxic clouds of religion, and all religions are focussed BACKWARDS to a

*This article acknowledges and relies on the findings of the Jesus Seminar, though it reaches its position from additional streams of study. It also assumes that the debate over the doctrines of the virgin birth, the miracles, and physical resurrection of Jesus are over, as are the debates on original sin, the Trinity, the literal interpretation of scripture, the notion of a God being a judgmental entity up in the heavens, and Jesus' death is a sacrifice to God for human sins.

claimed universal absolute authority for how people will live—
FORWARD.

Every day for the last forty years, I have sat with individuals and families who have had great difficulty in letting their hearts heal; they have experienced great pain and cannot let go of the past or move away from distressing memories.

Relationships in chaos, their dreams long since gone.
A young man with life potential hangs dead in the family garage.
A woman in her fifties molested by her teacher, uncle, or priest
forty years ago.
People, after Hiroshima and the Holocaust, pass on their tragic
grief from generation to generation.

Religion is powerless to help them—powerless perhaps because that religion has lost the essential connection with 'Him', the God who has been attributed as 'all-powerful'.

The bombs and bullets of war have been blessed with someone's quasi-religion. Someone's religious cocktail threw human minds into psychotic fear and guilt. History books have been extolled for their records of the horrors of our inhumanity, and only a page here and there was given over to those unsung heroes who created a little human happiness.

What we know is this: The religion of our distortions has repressed the God who somehow inspired someone to write:

Let people all over the earth make a joyful noise to the Lord.
(Psalm 100)

What we know is this: Many people have become mentally and spiritually wounded and paralyzed by life events, and in many instances their imposed religion keeps them there, believing it is God's will that they should suffer thus.

What we know is this: Many of us have become stuck in events and interpretations of the past, and we cannot, or do not, move on. We are no longer part of the vital streams that would carry us forward.

Some of you will remember the same rural scene as I knew in my youth. The winter rains would come. The streams would run. The gullies would flood, and the rivers would sweep down, carrying tons of rubbish and dead animals. Then we would notice a child's brightly coloured ball caught in the tangle at one bend in the river. There the ball stayed. Long after the full flood of the river had subsided, the ball remained stuck. There was nothing wrong with the ball. It was just no longer in-play.

Perhaps if Jesus of Nazareth were telling such a story, he might typically add a teaching — Take care lest you become like the ball in the river. The waters flow on, and you are left behind, alienated more each day from the energy of the river that once carried you so colourfully onwards. Take care lest you find yourself at one of life's impasses, and you become fixed in thought, mood, behaviour, and belief. Take care lest the colour of life fade from you as the colours fade from that ball!

If we take the story further we might say that the ball must wait for another flood or some other force to set it free, or it must accept its status at the bend of the river and bring what colour it can to the place where it has lodged. Perhaps Jesus, rather than giving the moral teaching, might say, "And this is what God's realm is like." It is to find yourself in a new context and find a transformed identity in that new context. That bend in the river can be just another bend in the river, or it can become the bend with the coloured ball for as long as the ball lasts.

In the full flow and floods of our life, and at every impasse and frustration we encounter, we try to find a meaningful, relevant faith—a New Faith. We know this: The Old Faith, the Old Religion has got itself jammed at the bend in the river and maintains that it is relevant to the flood that has long since left it behind. The Faith that was once supposed to bring us new life and a new way of being, a new connection with the God and Ground of our being, has been buried under the debris of many floods. Belief systems have bamboozled us, and complicated creeds have confused us. We have been carried along by rituals that have lost their relevance, and we have spent the centuries in church courts and councils locked in arguments of the impasse.

The New Faith contains a secret—God's secret. Our task is to crack the code. St Paul said, "I haven't yet found what I am looking for . . . but I press on toward the goal." (Phil 4:12–14).

We have a huge task, for people through the ages have tried to crack the code. Some have been absolutely convinced that they had the secret: Jesus Christ was the Saviour of the world. Others knew they had failed to crack the code. They saw that the code of Jesus Christ, Saviour of the world, had no compelling influence in a world of wars and drugs, of shocking tragedy, and of incurable suffering.

In the Old Testament Faith at its best, people knew the realities of human destruction and oppressive degradation of an existence stranded somewhere meaninglessly between what is and what could have been. But they could still formulate a Faith that says:

How beautiful upon the mountains are
The feet of the one who brings good tidings. (Isa 52:7)

They are words that unite the overriding themes of both the Old Testament and the New Testament, but we rarely, if ever, see the One, and all who promise to be carriers of good tidings confuse us with tangled logic or they conceal the code.

I have been trying to crack the code since I was four years of age. I lived on an isolated farm in the Australian bush. Church was miles away, so we never attended, except once a year—on harvest thanksgiving day. The congregation would swell from its normal five or six people to a "houseful" of forty people in a small redbrick church at three o'clock on a hot summer Sunday afternoon. My mother had tutored my brother and sisters in church behaviour, and I, being the youngest, received focussed attention. I was told that the minister would come in through a door behind the pulpit. He clearly had special status. And he would tell us all to say the Lord's Prayer, so we had to learn it.

I want you to go with that four-year-old into that awesome place amongst staring strangers. The pedal organ was no doubt squeezing out its strains, but all I remember is that the door behind the pulpit suddenly opened and in stepped that minister looking memorable in flowing black robes: surely this had to be 'God'. And then he called us to join in saying the Lord's Prayer. I immediately broke all earlier injunctions, grabbed hold of my mother, and said repeatedly in a loud voice: "I'm not saying it!"

That scene was a forerunner of a life-long search. Who and what was God? What words will we use to communicate with this God? What difference will it make? And in the washup of everything, does it matter?

I have been at St Michael's Church in the heart of Melbourne since 1971. Large numbers of people have come and gone, and come and gone. And if there is excitement to report it would take two forms: We have said we are searching for a New Faith, a New Way of understanding and appropriating, grasping, and shaping the meaning of God's Way, God's Realm, God's Kingdom.[1] Second, we are going to do this by integrating a therapeutic ministry with a preaching ministry, a communal psychology [2] with a relevant communal theology, an existential psychoanalysis with an existential religion.

Friedrich Nietzsche[3] startled his time by saying what we accept as common experience—we have killed the God we thought we owned. Rudolf Bultmann studied the New Testament and challenged us to find the substance under the layers of myth. Paul Tillich [4] in his obscure language focussed on Jesus of Nazareth pointing us to a New Being, the courage to be, in spite of the threats of nonbeing, and to a spiritual presence that was healing and transformative. Throughout Tillich's writing there was the demand for a Spiritual Intelligence of a kind we had not before known. Simultaneously, we embraced the challenge of Martin Buber[5] to find the way to a new humanity through dialogue and, through that dialogue, to a meeting with another dimension of life.

Through the ordinary 'thou' of human dialogue we were challenged to meet the 'Eternal Thou'.

Buber writes:

> We look out toward the fringes of the eternal THOU; in each we are aware of a breath from the eternal THOU; in each THOU we address the eternal THOU.

Through the manipulation and maneuvering in every collective, we were challenged to find the community.

The task was to crack the code[6] —to break through the impasse and apparent safety of our narcissism and to discover the way to the New Faith.

We came again to ask the vital question. Who was that Jesus of Nazareth, and what was he about?

Through the words and the events, here was someone pointing us to his God—the goodness at the heart of things, the gift of life itself, the enjoyment in the meeting, and the transforming healing presence. He was pointing to a new awareness of God often concealed in human interactions and human stories. (We might add—and concealed also in music, poetry, and art, in scientific discovery, and in philosophical and political debate.)

Martin Buber[7] reminded us that the process was one of an unfolding discovery rather than imposed dogma. Paul Tillich[8] said we were to engage in an existential inductive exploration of the human situation and to correlate that with an evolving understanding of the words of Jesus, rather than with an authoritarian deductive position that assumed God's secret was already fully disclosed, and then God's way only needed to be imposed.

Whether we are concerned with gambling, euthanasia, homosexuality, the role of women, or birth control, conventional religion had the definitive answer. The fact that Jesus did not state a view on any of these issues seemed of little concern. Conventional religion knows what God wants. It conveniently forgets what people in earlier centuries did in the name of God. In our time we are on heightened alert for terrorist attack. Imagine the slaughter of the Conquistadors: over twelve million deaths in the West Indies in the first forty years after Columbus sailed there.[9]

Conventional religion conveniently avoids the implications of dehumanisation. It speaks of the doctrine of original sin, without an adequate acceptance that the code is cracked only when we are involved in moving human beings to recognise their alienation from the best humanity and to find ways to a new creation, whatever that may mean.

Professor George Albee,[10] one-time president of the American Psychological Association, a nonbeliever who was once a guest in my pulpit, has said:

> All psychologists should help get rid of organised religion. It doesn't matter which religion; they are all patriarchal. And that is one of the major sources of social injustice in our society and in our world. Every major religion puts women down, grants women second-class status.

That should be enough for fifty percent of the population to question—even reject—these religions. Is it out of a fearful dependence that keeps them there? Are women destined by their gender to believe in a God that does not afford them equal status with the men with whom they sleep? We need to crack the code: What is this God like? Is it important?

Another distinguished visitor to my pulpit was the author and committed Roman Catholic, Morris West. I asked him if he believed in God. He eyed me cautiously and said, "It all depends whose God you are talking about. If you asked me if I believe in the God who is generally put before me from the pulpit, then I do not believe. If you mean the God I think the popes and cardinals espouse, I don't believe in that God". Then he opened his own book and read these words:

> Our Lord sat upon a hillside, perched himself in a rocking boat. The images he used were the simple images of rural life: flowers and sheep, grain and weeds (and) he taught his followers to acknowledge the unknown God as 'Father'.[11]

These words sound right, except they are enclosed unintentionally in the code—God is male, a father, a person. And as God is unknown, God is largely removed from many people's practical realities. We find that various polls can tell us what percentage of people believe in God, but if those believers have not cracked the code, God remains entrapped in the confusion of words and in the safety of unquestioned dogma and creed.

The male-person-father image of God in realistic terms requires a mother and a sexual union to produce a male son who was required to be genitally violated by circumcision without choice. Either we are speaking in code or we are having difficulty with the literalism of the language to the point where it is unbelievable and irrelevant.

 барожь барожь барожь

Many people cannot crack the code. They hate their tyrannical, abusive, demanding, and neurotic father. They live in a society that can in large numbers believe in God and deny the realities of domestic violence, pedophilia, sexual and sexist oppression, suicide, tobacco and drug addiction, damaged health, megadeaths per year, and, through all this, an existential emptiness and soul-lessness. The French-born psychoanalyst Julia Kristeva asks:

> Who still has a soul these days? . . . We have neither the time
> nor the space to create a soul for ourselves and the mere hint of
> such activity seems frivolous and ill-advised. [12]

I have given a lot of thought to the paintings and sculptures of Salvador Dali. Some people turn away from his distorted images believing that he was out of his mind. I don't think so. When he painted a clock melted out of shape, perhaps he was portraying how we lose the sense that this is our time and we miss claiming the moment as ours. One painting is of particular importance for us here—it is the landscape, utterly desolate, distorted, exhausted, and empty. Then through a small hole in the wall we see something in the distance. In this soul-less desert exists a presence. (*The Triangular Hour*)

In words attributed to Jesus and in events recorded about him, we see him telling stories that reached into the human soul in a transforming way to tell us about the God known as a presence. Author, Laura Simm writes: "We all need stories to break open our hearts and reconnect with the mystery of life."[13]

In our soul-lessness, in our soul deadness, and soul murder, we strive for that reconnection; we strive to crack the code and to make some sense of God's secret.

In all the stories surrounding Jesus of Nazareth we get a picture of the God to whom he was pointing us. There are six central signposts that tell us what we might find. If we want to know what God is like, we follow the signposts.

That four-year-old kid in that country church on a hot Sunday afternoon was overwhelmed by an awesome presence. It was a human presence, but to him it was a God-presence.

1. Jesus pointed to his God as a life-giving, life-enhancing, awesome, surprising presence.

A little girl at kindergarten painted her picture on a big sheet of white paper. It was the outline of a large square, in yellow paint.

The teacher came by, and pointing to the empty space inside the yellow square said, "What's in here?" The child replied, "I'm waiting for something." The teacher moved on. A little later the child filled the empty space with colours – red, green, purple, and orange.

Jesus of Nazareth could have said: "Suffer the little children and let them come to me, for of such is the heart and mind and joy of God."

Nikos Kazantzakis in *Zorba the Greek* writes: "God changes his appearance every second. Blessed is the (one) man who can recognise him in all his disguises."[14]

2. Jesus pointed to his God of affirming generosity, a God of invitation and inclusiveness. Many would head in other directions and towards their own chosen goals, but the fact of God's acceptance was there, all around them.

The Norwegian artist, Edvard Munch, is well known for his painting of the universal *Scream*. He has become known through that painting as the artist of depression and despair. But two other paintings of his hold my attention. One is the evening on the main street of Oslo. The street is crowded with people, their eyes bulging with anxiety, their faces frozen in emptiness. One person is walking against the crowd. He knows the others are heading the wrong way. The light of the parliament building is behind them and that's where they should be going. Or if only they would look up from their focussed delusion, they would see light all around them. It is as if they have succumbed to the narrow and deluded doctrine of their "original sin" and nothing will change them.

The second Munch painting (*Apple tree in the Garden*) is such a contrast; it is a surprise that this artist could accommodate such a dramatically different theme. It portrays two people in an orchard. The apple tree is loaded with beautiful fruit. The "original sin" motif has no place in the wider focus and context of this celebrative generosity. It seems to say, "See, the fruit in abundance is there without any deserving. Accept it and celebrate it".[15]

3. Jesus pointed to his God who would bring some healing to the human condition. Every child knows the plight of Humpty Dumpty. Every child knows the frustration of that one missing piece in a jigsaw puzzle. Every adult knows the emotional pain of distressing memories. Every person knows the gaps of life where nothing makes sense. Eugene O'Neill in *The Great God Brown*[16]

sees how our broken parts cry out for mending, and he says, "The grace of God is glue".

Jesus did not enter into complicated arguments about the place of suffering in the divine economy. We are thrown into life. Suffering and pain are the facts of life. With courage and some encouragement we cope, we create meanings, we evolve ways to lessen and prevent the pain and suffering.

Through it all we need "the glue" to hold us together, and we need to know we are "held" in what the psychoanalysts sometimes call "a holding environment".

Jesus pointed to his God who holds us in all of our failures and fragmentations, our sadness and suffering.

4. Jesus pointed to his God who opened people's eyes, opened rooftops, opened the doors of the wedding banquet—and those who were thus 'opened', became part of a new experience, a new life, a new being, and a new creation. We know how easily we settle for where we are, for the religion we always knew. Like the ball at the bend in the river, there are some who stay, though the river and all its mystery flows on.

Let us crack this code. It says this God opens us to a new spiritual intelligence. Let the psychologists speak to us of general intelligence, of social intelligence, and of emotional intelligence. Let us speak too — of a spiritual intelligence and its many specific ingredients and manifestations. The God to which Jesus pointed us keeps calling us FORWARD into an evolving spiritual intelligence that enriches life and growth.

D.H. Lawrence writes:

> As we live, we are transmitters of life,
> And when we fail to transmit life,
>   life fails to flow through us.

5. Jesus did not create a church nor did he speak of creating a church. He seemed to be a solitary wanderer searching for what God was like. He gathered people together, and in the gathering there was a listening wisdom, a nourishment of the human spirit, an expansion of the soul. His God was one who gathered people to listen and to be nourished in different ways from a solitary existence. We know we can be part of small and large gatherings and come and go without gain.

I like Honoré Daumier's painting called *The Third-Class Carriage*. It hangs in the New York Metropolitan Museum of Art. People are crowded into their train carriage. They take no notice of each other, and they are alone in their thoughts. (We have seen this many times!) The only thing they have in common is that they are traveling together. One carries a basket of food, but her eyes are empty. The movement of the train assures them they are going somewhere, but they probably do not realize that the 'basket' of their spirit is empty.

Compare that painting with Marc Chagall's *I and the Village*, which is full of imagination, memories of childhood, warmth, and colour. The act of milking a cow portrays an awesome world of life and giving. The painting explodes with the nourishment and enchantment of the human spirit.

Jesus pointed to his God of gathering, nourishment, enjoyment, and enchantment. The churches of our time need to study this signpost carefully.

The padre of the Australian outback, having ministered to scattered households for several years, was handing over to a young padre on his first posting. The older man knew his way through deserts and dry tracks, into properties and distant places. His advice to the young man who was about to begin the long journey was simple: "Always remember to shut the gates". The fence was necessary but not prohibitive. You can pass through the boundaries, but you must be sensitive and respectful of others and shut their gates.

> 6. Jesus pointed to his God that passed through all boundaries, necessary as they may be for some, but held each person's place and dignity as important.

Jesus seemed to say this was God's Way. He was a God of the journeys of life, recognising boundaries and transcending them, respecting individual dignity and space. 'God's Kingdom' is a code that needs to be cracked. It says we can all be part of God's Way—New Beings who recognise boundaries. But with courage, sensitivity, and respect we can transcend boundaries and leave the place a little better for having passed that way.

෨ ෨ ෨

Having said all of this, we need to pause and ponder that in the last century our wars have snuffed out the lives of sixty-five million civilians and forty-three million military personnel.[17] What other species claiming domination over all beasts and beings of every kind, and holding such conceptions of their God, would kill its own species in such numbers? At no point did Jesus of Nazareth say we should kill each other like this.

This horrifying human carnage takes no account of road deaths, smoking-related deaths, deaths from drugs, heart disease, cancers, and suicide.

Nearly two thousand years after Jesus of Nazareth, we cannot accept the equality of the sexes. We quarrel violently over homosexuality. Domestic violence, child abuse, pedophilia, and pornography conceal staggering statistics.

Why bother about a religion that is complicit in human degradation, about a God that has been displaced from that mythical throne in the heavens, about a church from which people have defected in large numbers?

From time to time, I hold a 'Talk-back' after morning service. People gather to ask questions or express views. Recently, a retired university vice-chancellor, who is a committed member of my church council , asked, "What then is worship? What is it we are doing and what difference does it make?"

We all know how church services can be so bland and boring, so unrelated to our personal situations, and so removed from the lowest levels of enjoyment, that we would not miss them if we never attended another one of them. So what is the point?

1. The four-year-old kid in the country church did not know what it was about, but he was in awe of something bigger than himself. As he sat in the congregation, his world expanded, and in his heart and mind he felt some excitement and anticipation. In the context of that gathering he saw the sheaves of hay, the bags of wheat, the pumpkins, the fruit, the vegetables. It was harvest festival. There was gratitude for this harvest that meant nourishment and survival. In the awareness of uncontrollable droughts, fire, and floods, there was also a sense of grace: along with hard work, there is added abundance.

Jesus the solitary wanderer, and he gathered people together to reconnect them with the God who was beyond them, and the God of Life and the Harvest. Worship is a gathering that the soul—individually and together—may be expanded in awe, affirmation, and expectation.

2. We use symbols to point to life and growth, colour and movement, helping people to identify with something larger than themselves, to walk taller in a spirit of transformation and transcendence. Symbols that conceal the code are used to crack the code.

One of the most dramatic symbols is portrayed in a sanctuary space on the west side of St Michael's church.[18] This space or room was once a formal chapel that is no longer used. We gutted it and built a sanctuary that holds huge sculptured rocks, which are symbols of the trauma of life and of returning stability and strength. People from the city and from other places in the world visit that space in their times of sadness and suffering. On Good Friday and remembrance days particularly, the whole congregation files past in absolute silence; they touch the rock, feel the water that flows over it, lift their eyes to the light, and in private thought and public action are at worship.

Wordsworth writes:

There are in our existence spots of time,
That with distinct pre-eminence retain
A renovating virtue, whence – depressed
By false opinion and contentious thought,
Or aught of heavier or more deadly weight,
In trivial occupations, and the round
Of ordinary intercourse – our minds
Are nourished and invisibly repaired,
A virtue, by which pleasure is enhanced,
That penetrates, enables us to mount,
When high, more high, and lifts us up when fallen.
(From *The Prelude – Imagination and Taste, How Impaired*
and Restored)

3. We sing hymns. Many hymns have words that we recognise publicly no longer reflect the New Faith, but there is an act of togetherness and music that brings us in touch with that side of humanity that has been widely lost—singing together.

4. With the scriptures I have long since used introductory words to relate Old Testament, Epistle, and Gospel passages that I have chosen for the theme of the service or the topic of the address. Invariably I rewrite and interpret the passages to put them into an understandable idiom. The various translations of the Bible are in a code that needs to be cracked.

In an attempt to break through the barrier of the scriptures being the sacred word, we have tried to emphasise first that the scriptures are not 'the word of God' nor are they totally inspired by God. The scriptures are words of 'men'. There are numerous examples where they exemplify a beautiful 'divine' inspiration, and there are further numerous examples where they are inspired by hate and fear.

We have attempted to get behind the manifest words to tap into the underlying hope and faith, and thereby present what the writer's best hopes were. Here are two examples of the way in which we have treated Psalm 21 and some verses of Ephesians 4.

Psalm 21

O God source of every breath,
    we celebrate the amazing gifts that come with our life.
We receive so much, and then you give us additional
    reasons to stop what we are doing, and celebrate.
We naturally wanted to live longer: you gave us
    more than longevity – you gave joy, vitality and fun.
We looked for things that gave us a sense of
    who we are, and you brought us a sense
    of your expansive presence.
We sought someone or something we could trust
    and you pointed us to the resilient strength
    of love and care.
We know there are events and influences that would
    make a mockery of the truly best things.
We know how the power of hate can threaten
    a good world.
Even our own anxieties and fears can become
    enemies that eat away our soul.
But we search for the pathways to the Good
    the True and the Beautiful[19] and we
    want to be on those pathways.
More than that we want to find ways
    to celebrate the enriching gifts you give us.

Ephesians 4:21–24, 30–32

You have been taught that the way of Christ is this –
Let go of what is now past, put aside all the destructiveness of your former ways, and start developing a new mind and a new spirit. Start developing a new nature which will be clearly seen by all as a life that really matters.

Get rid of all that persisting anger, the insults and malice;
    and be kind to each other
    cultivate a tender and generous heart
and practise accepting each other –
    as God has accepted you.

5. Similarly, we have wrestled with different ways in which to bring the congregation into corporate prayers. I have written three books of

prayers that attempt to be the relevant voice of the people at a particular time. Always there was the challenge of finding a way to address the One to whom the prayer was directed: "Almighty God", "Eternal Father", "Eternal Spirit". We have moved slowly away from the patriarchal anthropomorphic and genderised words for God. Ultimately we have come to words of "Good Spirit", "Spirit of Life", "Source of Life and Hope".

We have also gradually changed the endings of prayers to use less the mediating words of "through Jesus Christ our Lord", to words such as "This is our prayer", and then the people are invited to affirm that with their "Amen". An example follows:

> May the Great Mystery that we call God
>   keep alive in each one of us
>   the search for a Faith that is real
>   a Faith that helps us to live happier lives
>   a Faith that gives us a fuller
>   meaning to life and the events of life;
> Bring us to know the goodness that flows from
>   the heart of the universe, and may
>   we be expanded in heart and soul by
>   that goodness. This is our prayer.

Not so long ago, one of our men, 85 years of age, knew it was dying time. He had wrestled with his inner turbulence and had tried to settle for all time some of the outer stresses and neighbourly conflicts that had trailed through his life. He was in hospital struggling for breath and wanting to live a little longer until he could be sure he had reached his goal of contentment in heart and mind. In that context he took me by the hand and asked me where the Lord's Prayer was to be found in the Bible he held in his other hand. He wanted to revisit its meaning and understand how to integrate it into his dying state. His question contained three challenges. First, where to find the Lord's Prayer in his school-days Bible, its pages as thin as tissue paper and print so small no one could be ever expected to read it in a darkened hospital room, and I was without my spectacles. Second, I was to draw out an interpretation relevant to where he was at that moment. Third, I had to recognise that he wanted his personality to be in charge until he was finished with it. "Remember", he puffed, "my death is a result of my own stupidity, . . . I smoked heavily and I was stupid. How can I get over that?"

I reflected to myself that one of the characteristics of human neurosis is 'stupidity'. It sounds moralistic until we realise that being our own worst enemy is a little stupid. Repeating patterns we know will fail and acting

against our own best interests are things we all do — but they are manifestations of our stupidity. Oscar Wilde writes,

> "There is no sin except stupidity."

This is relevant to the Lord's Prayer especially as modern translations
enter into substituting words, like 'sins' for 'trespasses', and still retain a
conception of the God 'up there'.

So, bit by bit, I reinterpreted for the dying man the basic themes of
the Prayer:

> Good caring presence within us,
>   around us,
>   and above us;
> Hold us in a sense of mystery and wonder.
> Let the fullness of your goodness be within us
>   and around us;
> Let all the world know your ways of caring
>   and generosity.
> May we find we have all we need to meet
>   each day without undue anxiety.
> Overlook our many stupidities, and help us
>   to release everyone from their stupidities.
> May we all know we are accepted.
>   Strengthen us that we will reach out
>   to the best, always with the faith
>   to rise above the ugly realities of our existence.
> And we celebrate the gifts you have given us —
>   the rich kingdom of life's possibilities
>   the power to do good and the triumphs of good
>   and the moments when we have seen
>   the glory and wonder of everything.
> You are life's richness.
> You are life's power.
> You are life's ultimate meaning —
> Always — and for everyone — and for evermore.

In that faith, and in that deeply existential context, the man's personality transformed, he quietly died.

I told the Sunday morning congregation about it, and they have asked
again and again that they might say the prayer together.

For years I retained the conventional wording of the Communion where we were exhorted to eat the flesh and drink the blood of another human being. I referred to this at my church council until one of them said, "For goodness' sake and for ours, change it". So I did. Instead of speaking of Jesus suffering for us and dying for us, I take the bread and wine and hold them up as symbols of life, nurture, and strength for our living in all the exigencies of our fragmented existence.

The address fits the historic fact that St Michael's has always been a preaching church—for the most part with a liberal or popular content. In my watch, I have overtly sought to combine a high level of psychoanalytic experience with a thorough searching of a biblical existential theology. People are attracted to the Sunday service by the title of the address advertised in the Saturday papers and by their awareness of the evolving record of the congregation. The topic titles are aimed at the readers' needs and seek to articulate dormant issues in society:

> Your search for a higher spiritual intelligence.
> Strong answers to your existential questions.
> Strange things happen and sometimes we are stronger.
> Sooner or later, we all adapt. But what is the best way?
> Six central teachings of Christianity.
> Our search for a safe world.
> How your personality can change for the better.
> The Spirit within needs to be nourished; then it nourishes everything.
> Rehumanising a dehumanised society.
> Our huge moral dilemmas.
> Conventional religion! Who needs it? Five breakthroughs to a different Faith.
> Three things at Christmas: A bunch of marigolds, some old newspaper, *and you.

These addresses attempt to reflect the positive, prevailing, rich, and powerful images of God and the way of Faith to help and enhance people's self-perception and potential, and their participation in the evolution and growth towards a better humanity. This is done by evocative, engaging teaching and through images and stories that are likely to be both affirming and realistically optimistic in their portrayal of the place of Faith for happiness, health, and well-being.

The service ends with the blessing. I can no longer accept the concept of the creedal trinity. I am sure that people in the congregation could never understand its relevance to them. So I say:

> May the God you see in all the colours of creation
>   arouse in you a sense of awe and wonder.
> May the God who is a sacred presence be real to you.
> May the God who is a source of inspiration
>   and courage keep calling you forward.
> May your God go with you, and bless you.

We are part of the vital process of bringing forward a new perspective and understanding. We are breaking ancient codes to discover a meaning for our situations in life.

I hear this challenge expressed in the inspirational music of Mahler's Fifth Symphony. Listen to the fourth movement and its doleful, echoing, searching cadences of the horns that take us on the uncertain distant journey. Is this what life is about? The horns fade away, and we are left with the plucking of the strings. It seems as if it is all over, when through the empty darkness the Adagietto of the fifth movement comes in all its exquisite tenderness, its embracing assurance of a gentler world, soothing the most turbulent anxiety.

Perhaps in that moment, the code begins to crack.

A longstanding friend, who was one of Melbourne's distinguished psychiatrists until he died, and a pioneer of a nonreligious therapeutic-meditation movement, and a poet, wrote:

> A new light
> Shines on old celebrations
> New meaning comes
> Which we did not have before.[20]

We have not fully cracked the code, but we are part of that new meaning that the New Faith opens for us.

Notes

The Art of Gaining and Losing Everything
Roy W. Hoover

1 Paul S. Minear, *The Bible and the Historian*.

2 Minear, p. 27.

3 Cited in Minear, pp. 28 and 27.

4 Minear, p. 27.

5 Minear, p. 28.

6 Pelikan, *Bach Among Theologians*, p. 133.

7 Minear, p. 34.

8 Cp. Luke 17:33 and parallels.

9 Those scholars who have labored so prodigiously to deny that Paul was converted to a new faith as well as called to a new vocation are mistaken, in my view.

10 See Paul's sharp-tongued remarks in Philippians 3:2–11.

11 Tarnas, *The Passion of the Western Mind*, p. 416.

12 For a well-written and substantive account of the history of American religionists' responses to this challenge, see William R. Hutchison, *The Modernist Impulse*.

13 Kaufman, *In Face of Mystery*, p. 433.

14 Cp. 2 Corinthians 5:16. This reconstructed paraphrase of Paul's remark reflects the radical difference between ancient and modern worldviews.

15 Cited in Hutchison, *Modernist*, pp. 223–24.

16 Cited in Hutchison, *Modernist,* p. 224.

17 Cited in Hutchison, *Modernist,* p. 224.

18 The authors of this fiction are really the ones who have been *left behind*—by the modern world.

19 Niebuhr, *Christian Ethics*, 32 [italics added]. My remarks in this paragraph are also drawn from Niebuhr's on pp. 19 and 35; and *Nature and Destiny*, II, p. 72.

20 Niebuhr, *Faith and History*, p. 127.

21 *Faith and History*, p. 128 [italics added].

22 *Faith and History*. p. 131.

23 Paul Tillich's discussion of "The Symbol 'Kingdom of God' as the Answer to the Question of the Meaning of History" remains pertinent and useful, despite criticism of his theological system as a whole. See his *Systematic Theology*, vol. 3, pp. 356–61.

24 Cp. the remarks of Gordon Kaufman, *Mystery*, pp. 223–24. One might say

that developing the implications of this point is what Kaufman's whole book is about.,

25 "Good News." Unsigned editorial in *The Christian Century*, November 20— December 3, 2002, p. 5.

26 Miroslav Volf, "Way of Life," p. 35.

27 This way of referring to modern conceptions of the universe and the human person are taken from Kaufman, *Mystery*, p. 429.

28 Modeled on Kaufman's remarks in *Mystery*, p. 430.

29 Church members would also be enlightened and inspired if they learned how the church decided what to include in the New Testament. For a brief readable account see my article, "How the Books of the New Testament Were Chosen," or "How the Canon Was Determined."

More ambitious readers would do well to consult Harry Y. Gamble, *The New Testament Canon*. Avid readers will find a substantial discussion in Lee M. McDonald, *The Formation of the Christian Biblical Canon*.

30 The phrasing of this statement is modeled on a similar remark by Gerd Luedemann in *The Resurrection of Jesus*, p. 180.

31 Kaufman, *Mystery*, p. 437.

If You Give a Mouse a Cookie...
Stephen J. Patterson

1 Laura Joffe Numeroff, *If You Give a Mouse a Cookie* (New York: Harper Collins, 1985).

2 Michael Castle, "In the Midst of New Dimensions" (Unpublished Thesis, Eden Theological Seminary, 2001).

3 Marcus Borg has distinguished between "natural literalism" and the "conscious literalism" of modern American fundamentalism ("The Jesus Seminar and the Church," in Borg, *Jesus in Contemporary Scholarship*, pp. 174–77).

4 The term Open and Affirming designates congregations in the United Church of Christ that are self-consciously open to and affirming of gay, lesbian, bi-sexual, and transgendered people.

5 Castle, pp. 48–50. For some in Castle's church, "the Bible had authority because it derived from God. It was the 'rule book' and the 'answer book' for Christian faith and practice. Because of its origins in God, the Bible could be trusted to tell the truth about life, faith, and Jesus" (pp. 49–50).

6 "New Testament and Mythology," pp. 1–44 in Rudolf Bultmann, *New Testament and Mythology*.

7 Koester, "Writings and the Spirit."

8 The earliest printed documents are probably to be dated in the 1440s, somewhat before Gutenburg's most famous print achievement, the *Latin Bible of 42 lines*, which appeared sometime in 1456.

9 Castle, 68–94. As Castle puts it: "Jesus' power is inextricably tied to God, so that the ultimate question of power is centered not in Jesus, but in God" (p. 69).

10 Of the hundreds who have approached the problem, I find Charles Hartshorne to be especially insightful in *Omnipotence and Other Theological Mistakes*.

11 Op. Imp. III, 7, as noted by Peter Brown, *Augustine of Hippo*, p. 393. The context was Augustine's dispute with Julian of Eclanum, who had regarded Augustine's

ideas about original sin as barbaric and failing even the most basic test of justice. Julian, by contrast, argued of view of God based on traditional ideas of justice and fairness in the best Roman legal tradition. He supported his view with a cultivated naiveté about the Bible, finding in it "no pockets of primitive vengeance, no supports for theories of blood guilt" (Brown, p. 393). Augustine's view at least had the merit of taking in more of the rough edges of the biblical tradition.

12 Brown, *Augustine of Hippo, p. 393*, citing C. *Jul.* VI, pp. 25, 82

13 "Can Schweitzer Save Us from Russell?" as cited by Richard Wightman Fox, *Reinhold Niebuhr*, p. 102.

14 Mark 10:21, pars.

15 Gos Thom 55, pars.

16 Q 12:51 (Luke 12:51//Matt 10:34), pars.

American Churches and the Culture Wars
Lane C. McGaughy

1 Quoted in Harland, p. 80.
2. Quoted in Harland, p. 85.
3. Howell, pp. 75–81.

Learning to See God
Joe Bessler-Northcutt

1 By skepticism, I don't mean to lay claim to the epistemological tradition that argues we cannot have sure knowledge of either things or other persons. Rather, I intend a stance that is suspicious of those totalizing fundamentalist and orthodox religious visions that proclaim a definitive Truth—silencing all doubts and requiring faithful submission as the price of salvation. I mean instead a stance that acknowledges and owns the deep ambiguity that accompanies all human relating, including thinking.

2 For a discussion of the play on "knowledge" and "acknowledgment," see Stanley Cavell, *The Claim of Reason*, especially Part Four, pp. 329–496, and *The Senses of Stanley Cavell*, edited by Richard Fleming and Michael Payne, especially James Conant, "An Interview with Stanley Cavell," pp. 21–72, and Richard Eldridge's "'A Continuing Task': Cavell and the Truth of Skepticism," pp. 73–89.

3 *Thomas Merton: Spiritual Master*, p. 375.

4 *Thomas Merton: Spiritual Master*, p. 374.

5 For a good discussion of theological response to that biblical scholarship, see John Hick, *The Metaphor of God Incarnate*, especially chapter three, "From Jesus to Christ."

6 Arguing about the Q gospel's theology, John Kloppenborg Verbin writes: "The center of Q's theology is not Christology [that is, claims about Jesus' status, such as Messiah, Lord, Son of God] but the reign of God." *Excavating Q*, p. 391, 392.

7 Such readings throughout Christian history have utterly refused to lay Jesus' teaching alongside the realities of his social world. Because the metaphysical assumptions of Jesus' divine identity required an ultimately mythological context, the kingdom of God *had* to be extra-historical.

8 Richard Horsley and Neil Asher Silberman, *The Message and the Kingdom*, p. 55.

9 Stephen J. Patterson, *The God of Jesus*, p. 64.

10 Patterson, pp. 69–87.

11 On the difference between the two, see Bernard Brandon Scott, *Hear Then the Parable*, pp. 56–62.

12 For the kingdom, or empire of God" as ironic discourse see Bernard Brandon Scott, *Re-Imagine the World*, p. 135.

13 Scott also suggests that Jesus' rhetorical choice of the term "kingdom" ultimately betrayed him. See *Re-Imagine the World*, pp. 135–37.

14 Richard Rorty, *Philosophy and the Mirror of Nature*.

15 Bernard Brandon Scott, *Hear Then the Parable*, (Minneapolis, Fortress Press, 1989), p. 194.

16 See notes #1 and #2 above.

17 See Scott's discussion in *Hear Then the Parable*, pp. 197–200.

18 Funk & Hoover, *The Five Gospels*, p. 152.

19 Funk & Hoover, *The Five Gospels*, p. 153.

20 Scott, *Re-Imagine the World*, p. 34.

21 Given my critique of God as supreme being, some might wonder why insist on God-language at all. I think the question would have missed much of my point. Just as Jesus inherited a tradition that he turned and shaped rhetorically, so do we. Just as Jesus did not think that integrity meant rejecting his tradition but critically engaging it (a process that Cavell calls "inheriting a tradition" (see note #1 above)), so I believe God-language is utterly vital for articulating a skeptical stance toward political and cultural injustice and for naming that transcendently elusive and immanently glimpsed joy of belonging to a just and compassionate world.

22 For several now-classic criticisms of omnipotent and kingly metaphors for God see Gordon D. Kaufman, *Theology in a Nuclear Age*, and Sallie McFague's *Models of God*.

23 *Thomas Merton: Spiritual Master*, p. 144.

24 One finds a similar concern from a Buddhist perspective in Thich Nhat Hanh's *A Guide to Walking Meditation*, which encourages the practice of mindfulness in the midst of one's active life.

25 See, for example, Kay Bessler Northcutt, "August in Her Breast: Prayer as Embodiment," pp. 205–218.

26 I have found Lewis Mudge's book, *The Sense of a People*, quite suggestive along these lines.

The Search for Community and the Historical Jesus
Hal Taussig

1 The first of these essays was my profile of the historical Jesus, recently published in *Profiles of Jesus*, but written some four years ago for the Seminar. In that first essay, I concluded that "some significance for the historical Jesus can be asserted," (p. 35) but that "the religious and intellectual significance of this historical Jesus is consistently overstated." (35) The second essay, "History Matters: A Postmodern Case for Jesus and Meaning Today," (written for the Once and Future Faith Conference for the Spring 2001 meeting) took on the challenge of what kind of

significance the historical Jesus may have for today, and proposed a way of framing meaning-making about the historical Jesus, using the literary categories of *ethos*, *muthos*, and *dianoia* in the work of Northrop Frye (pp. 117–33). The third essay (written for the Fall 2001 meeting), "Transfiguring Jesus: An Assessment of the Spiritual Dimensions of Contemporary Historical Jesus Portraits," (pp. 41–53) identified seven spiritual characteristics of the historical Jesus in contemporary historical Jesus scholarship. This essay proposed a methodology for working on the spiritual significance of the historical Jesus, which can be summarized in the following agenda: "we need to pursue our historical critical work, admit and proclaim consciously the spiritual context and results of our articulations about the historical Jesus, accept and name as best we can our particular subjectivities and social locations, submit ourselves to critique especially by those interested in Jesus from different socio-cultural perspectives, and welcome the larger collective and public energy for Jesus as belonging to our work itself." (p. 52)

2 This paragraph is quoted in full from Nerney and Taussig, *Re-Imagining Life Together in America*, p. xviii.

3 Most of the preceding five paragraphs are taken directly from Nerney and Taussig, *Re-Imagining Life Together in America*, beginning with "That early Christians were excited..." through "an abstract, non-communal message about God." (7, 8)

4 The preceding two paragraphs are taken directly from Nerney and Taussig, *Re-Imagining Life Together in America*, p. 23.

5 Cf. my "History Matters: A Postmodern Case for Jesus and Meaning Today," (written for the Once and Future Faith Conference for the Spring 2001, meeting) and "Transfiguring Jesus: An Assessment of the Spiritual Dimensions of Contemporary Historical Jesus Portraits," (written for the Fall 2001 meeting) for other dimensions of meaning-making around the historical Jesus today.

6 Cf. both his *The Historical Jesus* and *Jesus: A Revolutionary Biography*.

7 When discussing the character of Jesus' relationship to those he taught, scholars seem more comfortable with the word "movement" than "group" or "community." Cf. Crossan, *The Historical Jesus*, pp. 8–43, 282–323.

8 See the summary in Funk, *The Five Gospels*, pp. 10–25.

9 Cf. a number of portraits of such churches in *Re-Imagining Life Together*, pp. 165–236.

The Jesus Seminar in Africa
Glenna S. Jackson

1 Everyone's experience is different, of course. One example is our colleague and fellow in the Jesus Seminar, Andries van Aarde, who literally has been through two heresy trials as a result of his historical Jesus research and his involvement in the Jesus Seminar at the University of Pretoria in South Africa.

2 Mwombeki, "Reading the Bible in Contemporary Africa."

3 Pui-lan, "Discovering the Bible in the Non-Biblical World: The Journey Continues," *Journal of Asian and Asian American Theology* as quoted in Pui-lan, "Jesus/The Native: Biblical Studies from a Postcolonial Perspective," p. 69.

4 Bakare, *My Right to Land*, pp. 31–33. My students agreed with the red color of that parable.

5 Bakare, p. 36.

6 Bakare, p. 39.

7 Bakare, p.39, from Crossan, *In Parables*, p. 33.

8 Arland J. Hultgren, *The Parables of Jesus*, p. 411.

9 Jackson, "The Complete Gospel," 27–39, and "Jesus as First-Century Feminist," 85–98.

10 Mwombeki, pp. 127–28. I am indebted to Owen K. Ross ("The Main Reasons for a New Approach To Do Theology in Africa," [Mutare, Zimbabwe: Africa University class paper, 2000]) for his bibliography on the subject: Canaan Sodindo Banana, *The Church and the Struggle for Zimbabwe: From the Programme To Combat Racism To Combat Theology* (Gweru, Zimbabwe: Mambo Press, 1996); Michel Chossudovsky, *The Globalisation of Poverty: Impacts of IMF and World Bank Reforms* (Malaysia: Third World Network, 1997); Lual A. Deng, *Rethinking African Development: Toward a framework for social integration and ecological harmony* (Asmara: African World Press, 1998); Peter Kasenene, *Religious Ethics in Africa* (Kampala: Fountain Press, 1998); Emmanuel Martey, *African Theology: Inculturation and Liberation* (Maryknoll: Orbis Books, 1993); John S. Mbiti, *Introduction to African Religion* (Harare: Heinemann, 1989); John Parratt, *Reinventing Christianity: African Theology Today* (Grand Rapids, MI: Eerdmans, 1995).

11 Dube, "'Go Therefore and Make Disciples of All Nations,'" p. 243.

The "Good News" about the Historical Jesus
Charles W. Hedrick

1 Wallace Stevens, "Cy est pourtraicte, madam ste Ursule, et les unze mille vierges," p. 22; ["Here is an image: Lady Saint Ursule, and the eleven thousand virgins."]

2 I am using the term "church" in a broad institutional sense to include the many diverse groups associated with the Christian tradition.

3 The "Historical Jesus" is Jesus of Nazareth as he may be described by using the same historical criteria we would use in describing any figure of history.

4 See Charles H. Dodd, *The Apostolic Preaching*.

5 See Henry Bettenson and Chris Maunder, *Documents of the Christian Church*.

6 Even if the recently discovered ossuary turns out to be authentic, it tells us nothing we did not already know. So if authentic, it will likely turn out to be merely a "holy relic." See André Lemaire, "Earliest Archeological Evidence," and Hershel Shanks, "The Storm over the Bone Box," pp. 26–39, 83.

7 Only three fragmentary Christian manuscripts are dated as early as the second century: two fragments of the Gospel of John, and the Egerton Gospel.

8 See Bart D. Ehrman, *The Orthodox Corruption of Scripture*.

9 For an accessible statement of the problem see Charles W. Hedrick, *When History and Faith Collide*.

10 See Bettenson and Maunder, *Documents*, pp. 25–29.

11 The history of the quest for the Jesus of history may be read in two books: Albert Schweitzer, *The Quest of the Historical Jesus*, and Walter P. Weaver, *The Historical Jesus in the Twentieth Century*.

12 Dodd, *Apostolic Preaching*, 11; compare 1 Cor 15:3 and Gal 1:4.

13 Dodd, *Apostolic Preaching*, p. 17.

14 Dodd, *Apostolic Preaching*, pp. 25–26. Dodd, however, minimizes the signifi-cance of these differences. There were other kerygmas; I cite these two because they were part of orthodox traditions.

15 Marion L. Soards, "Paul" in Mills et al., *Mercer Dictionary of the Bible*, p. 662.

16 Hedrick, *When History and Faith Collide*, p. 14.

17 Stephen L. Harris, *The New Testament*, p. 311.

18 To be sure, the early church was well aware that Jesus was a human being (see Dodd, *Apostolic Preaching*, 29), but his personal history is not what was really impor-tant about him. Hence the only aspects of his personal history to be included in orthodox kerygmas, according to Dodd, were his birth, death, and burial.

19 For the early creeds of the church see Bettenson and Maunder, *Documents of the Christian Church*, pp. 25–29.

20 The barest reference to Jesus' career appears in the Jerusalem kerygma: his deeds (Acts 2:22) and his words (Acts 3:22). See Dodd, *Apostolic Preaching*, pp. 21–22.

21 For example, compare the diversity among the canonical gospels: *When History and Faith Collide*, pp. 30–75, and see the classic study by Walter Bauer, *Orthodoxy and Heresy*.

22 The only other times the word "sign" is used in Mark is in 13:4, when Jesus is asked about a sign for the destruction of the temple and in 13:22, where Jesus warns about false messiahs who "do signs and wonders."

23 See also Matt 16:1–4, where Matthew again has Jesus give the sign of Jonah, but this time without an interpretation.

24 See Hedrick, *When History and Faith Collide*, pp. 42 and 51, #2.

25 R. Douglas Geivett completely ignores the problems posed by the disjunction between mythology and modern science when he affirms the Apostles Creed as distilling "the outline of a total package of orthodox New Testament belief": "Is Jesus the only way," p. 180. By not at least acknowledging the difficulties, his paper is intellectually dishonest.

26 See my discussion of this issue in Hedrick, *When History and Faith Collide*, pp. 1–13.

27 The narrator of the Gospel of John appears to be the only canonical gospel to claim direct access to eyewitness testimony in some form (John 19:35 and 20:24), though it may well be an appeal to tradition, which the author believed to be based on eyewitness testimony. Luke's observation about eyewitnesses (1:2) appears to be an appeal to tradition, which Luke regarded as based on eyewitness testimony.

28 This kind of information seems to be the kind of testimony John claims to have available.

29 See Hedrick, *When History and Faith Collide*, pp. 110–34.

30 See Hedrick, *When History and Faith Collide*, pp. 135–52.

31 Robert W. Funk and Roy W. Hoover, eds., *The Five Gospels*.

32 Robert W. Funk, ed., *The Acts of Jesus*.

33 Roy W. Hoover, *Profiles of Jesus*.

34 The consensus may change on the basis of historical argument, and sayings may be added to the data, but it is unlikely that the data will be reduced by much.

35 Obviously this is my personal opinion, but one based on my profile of the his-torical Jesus: see "Jesus of Nazareth. A Profile under Construction" in Hoover, *Profiles of Jesus*.

36 See Hedrick, *When History and Faith Collide*, pp. 1–13.

37 See Charles W. Hedrick, "Miracle Stories as Literary Compositions."

38 See Charles W. Hedrick, Jr., *History and Silence*, pp. 37–88: "After about 440, no further pagans are attested among the elite of the city of Rome" (p. 57). Earlier (341) the sons of Constantine, Constans and Constantius II, had attempted to abolish pagan sacrifice and close pagan temples (see Hedrick, *History and Silence*, 40); for the text, see A. D. Lee, *Pagans and Christians*, p. 96.

39 In 313 Constantine exempted Christian clergy from public duties and restored church property that had been seized in earlier persecutions: for the texts see Bettenson and Maunder, *Documents*, 16–19. See also the provocative essay by Keith Hopkins, "Christian Number and Its Implications," particularly pages pp. 222–26.

40 See Lee, *Pagans and Christians in Late Antiquity*, pp. 132–48.

41 The problem of New Testament mythology is not new for pastors; it is just late in getting to the pew. Pastors do not always come clean with their parishioners. See Rudolf Bultmann, "New Testament Mythology," pp. 1–16 in Hans Werner Bartsch, ed., *Kerygma and Myth*; Karl Jaspers and Rudolf Bultmann, *Myth and Christianity*; and John A. T. Robinson, *Honest to God*. Bultmann was a German Lutheran academic who preached and Robinson was an Anglican churchman (Bishop of Woolwich).

42 Plutarch reports that near the Greek island of Paxi an unknown caller cried out to a passing ship for the pilot, one Thamus, an Egyptian, to announce "that Great Pan is dead" when the ship came near the island of Palodes. Thamus made the announcement, and immediately those on the ship heard a great lamentation of many voices. See Plutarch, *Moralia*, 419 c-d: Frank Cole Babbitt, *Plutarch's Moralia*, V. pp. 400–403.

43 See Hedrick, *When History and Faith Collide*, xi-xiii.

44 See, for example, 1 Tim 3:16; 1 Cor 4:1; 1 Tim 3:9; Eph 6:19–20; Col 2:2, 4:3.

45 Robert W. Funk, *A Credible Jesus*.

46 For the comments that follow, see my paper "Jesus of Nazareth. A Profile Under Construction" in Hoover, *Profiles of Jesus*.

47 See the collection of essays in Armstrong et al., *The Once and Future Jesus*.

Preaching The New Faith
Francis Macnab

1 Funk, R. (2000) Once and Future Faith. St Michael's Uniting Church, Melbourne.

2 Sometimes referred to as 'community psychology' or 'community psychotherapy'

3 Nietzsche, F. *Thus Spake Zarathustra*.

4 Tillich, P. *Systematic Theology*.

5 Buber, M., *I and Thou*, Friedman, M., *Martin Buber*.

6 I thank Patsie Stubbs for this concept. She is for many years a member of St Michael's. She said to me – "I see what you are doing. You are out to 'crack the code'".

7 Buber, M. *I and Thou*.

8 Tillich, P., *Systematic Theology*.

9 See Young, R. "Fundamentalism as Terrorism."

10 Albee, G. quoted by Bridget Murray, "Same Office, Different Aspirations, " p. 20.

11 West, M., A *View From The Bridge*, p. 8

12 Kristeva, J. (1995) *Maladies of the Soul*.

13 Simm, Laura., p. 53

14 Kazantzakis, N. *Zorba The Greek*.

15 Prelinger, E., *After the Scream*.

16 O'Neill, E. *The Great God Brown*.

17 See Hedges, C. *War is a Force That Gives Us Meaning*. He gives first hand accounts of many wars.

18 It's called Mingary – a Gaelic place name from the Isle of Mull. It is a place of nurture and safety, a place evoking the desire to go on further.

19 See Wilber, K., *The Marriage of Sense and Soul*.

20 Meares, A., *From the Quiet Place*.

Works Consulted

Ahlstrom, Sidney E. *A Religious History of the American People*. New Haven and London: Yale University Press, 1972.

Armstrong, Karen et al. *The Once and Future Jesus*. Santa Rosa, CA: Polebridge Press, 2000.

Babbitt, Frank. Phutarch's Moralia. Cambridge: Harvard University Press, 1962.

Bakare, Sebastian. *My Right to Land—in the Bible and in Zimbabwe: A Theology of Land in Zimbabwe*. Harare: Zimbabwe Council of Churches, 1993.

Banana, Canaan Sodindo. *The Church and the Struggle for Zimbabwe: From the Programme To Combat Racism To Combat Theology*. Gweru, Zimbabwe: Mambo Press, 1996.

Bartsch, Hans Werner, ed., *Kerygma and Myth. A Theological Debate*. New York: Harper & Row, 1961.

Bauer, Walter. *Orthodoxy and Heresy in Earliest Christianity*. Eds. Robert A Kraft and Gerhard Krodel. Philadelphia: Fortress, 1971 (First ed. 1934).

Bellah, Robert. "Civil Religion in America." *Religion in America*. Eds. William McLoughlin and Robert Bellah. Boston: Beacon Press, 1966.

Bellah, Robert. "Reforming our Institutions of Meaning." *Fugitive Faith: Conversations on Spiritual, Environmental, and Community Renewal*. Ed. Benjamin Webb. Maryknoll, NY: Orbis Books, 1998.

Bellah, Robert. "Religion and the Shape of National Culture." *America* 181,3 (1999).

Bellah, Robert et al. *Individualism and Commitment in American Life: Readings on the Themes of Habits of the Heart*. New York: Harper and Row, 1987.

Bellah, Robert, et al. *Habits of the Heart: Individualism and Commitment in American Life*. Berkeley and Los Angeles: University of California Press, 1985.

Bessler Northcutt, Kay. "August in Her Breast: Prayer as Embodiment." *Setting the Table: Women in Theological Conversation*. Eds. Rita Nakashima Brock, Claudia Camp, and Serene Jones. St. Louis, MO: Chalice Press, 1995.

Bettenson, Henry, and Chris Maunder, eds. *Documents of the Christian Church*. Third ed. Oxford: Oxford University Press, 1999.

Borg, Marcus. *Jesus in Contemporary Scholarship*. Valley Forge: Trinity Press International, 1994.

Brown, Peter. *Augustine of Hippo: A Biography*. Berkeley and Los Angeles: University of California Press, 1967.

Brown, Raymond. *The Community of the Beloved Disciple: The Life, Loves, and Hates of an Individual Church in New Testament Times*. Mahwah, NJ: Paulist Press, 1979.

Buber, Martin. *I and Thou*. Edinburgh: T. & T. Clarke, 1937.

Bultmann, Rudolf. "New Testament and Mythology." *New Testament and Mythology and Other Basic Writings*. Ed. and Trans. Schubert Ogden. Philadelphia: Fortress Press, 1984.

Castle, Michael. "In the Midst of New Dimensions." Ph.D. diss., Eden Theological Seminary, 2001.

Cavell, Stanley. *The Claim of Reason: Wittgenstein, Skepticism, Morality, and Tragedy*. New York: Oxford University Press, 1979.

Crossan, J. Dominic. *The Historical Jesus: The Life of a Mediterranean Jewish Peasant*. San Francisco: HarperSanFrancisco, 1991.

Crossan, J. Dominic. *In Parables: The Challenge of the Historical Jesus*. Sonoma, CA: Polebridge Press, 1992.

Crossan, J. Dominic. *Jesus: A Revolutionary Biography*. San Francisco: HarperCollins, 1994.

Dodd, C. H. *The Apostolic Preaching and its Developments*. Second ed. New York: Harper & Brothers, 1944 [1st ed. 1936]).

Dube, Muse, "'Go Therefore and Make Disciples of All Nations' (Matt 28:19a)." *Teaching the Bible: The Discourses and Politics of Biblical Pedagogy*. Eds. Fernando F. Segovia and Mary Ann Tolbert. Maryknoll, NY: Orbis Books, 1998.

Ehrman, Bart D. *The Orthodox Corruption of Scripture. The Effect of Early Christological Controversies on the Text of the New Testament*. Oxford: Oxford University Press, 1993.

Fleming, Richard, and Michael Payne, eds. *The Senses of Stanley Cavell*. Cranbury, NJ: Associated University Presses, 1989.

Friedman, Maurice. *Martin Buber: The Life of Dialogue*. Chicago: University of Chicago Press, 1955.

Funk, Robert W. *A Credible Jesus: Fragments of a Vision*. Santa Rosa, CA: Polebridge Press, 2002.

Funk, Robert W. and the Jesus Seminar. *The Acts of Jesus: The Search for the Authentic Words of Jesus*. San Francisco: HarperCollins, 1998.

Funk, Robert W., Roy W. Hoover, and the Jesus Seminar. *The Five Gospels: The Search for the Authentic Words of Jesus*. San Francisco: HarperSanFrancisco, 1993.

Gamble, Harry Y. *The New Testament Canon. Its Making and Meaning*. Philadelphia: Fortress Press, 1985.

Gaustad, Edwin Scott. *A Religious History of America*. New York: Harper & Row, 1966.

Geivett, R. Douglas. "Is Jesus the only way." Pp. 177–205 in *Jesus Under Fire*. Eds. Michael J. Wilkins and J. P. Moreland. Grand Rapids: Zondervan, 1995.

"Good News." Unsigned editorial in *The Christian Century* (November 20—December 3, 2002): 5.

Harland, Gordon. "The American Protestant Heritage and the Theological Task." *The Drew Gateway* XXXII,2 (Winter 1962): 71–93.

Harris, Stephen L. *The New Testament: A Student's Introduction*. Fourth ed. Boston: McGraw Hill, 2002.

Hartshorne, Charles. *Omnipotence and Other Theological Mistakes*. Albany: State University of New York, 1984.

Hedges, C. *War is a Force That Gives Us Meaning*. New York: Public Affairs, 2002.

Hedrick, Charles W. "Miracle Stories as Literary Compositions: The Case of Jairus' Daughter." *Perspectives in Religious Studies* 20.3 (1993): 217–33.

Hedrick, Charles W. *When History and Faith Collide. Studying Jesus.* Peabody, MA: Hendrickson, 1999.

Hedrick, Jr., Charles W. *History and Silence. Purge and Rehabilitation of Memory in Late Antiquity.* Austin: University of Texas Press, 2000.

Herberg, Will. *Protestant-Catholic-Jew: An Essay in American Religious Sociology.* Garden City, NY: Doubleday & Company, 1955; Anchor edition, 1960.

Hick, John. *The Metaphor of God Incarnate.* Louisville: Westminster John Knox Press, 1993.

Hoover, Roy W. "How the Books of the New Testament Were Chosen," in *Approaches to the Bible. The Best of* Bible Review. Biblical Archaeology Society, 1994, I, 114–20.

Hoover, Roy W. "How the Canon Was Determined." *The Fourth R* 5, 1 (January 1992): 1–7.

Hoover, Roy W., ed. *Profiles of Jesus.* Santa Rosa, CA: Polebridge Press, 2002.

Hopkins, Keith. "Christian Number and Its Implications," *Journal of Early Christian Studies* 6.2 (1998): 185–226.

Horsley, Richard and Neil Asher Silberman. *The Message and the Kingdom: How Jesus and Paul Ignited a Revolution and Transformed the Ancient World.* Minneapolis: Fortress Press, 1997.

Howell, Leon. *United Methodism @ Risk: A Wake-Up Call.* Kingston, NY: Information Project for United Methodists, 2003.

Hudson, Winthrop S. *Religion in America.* New York: Charles Scribner's Sons, 1965.

Hultgren, Arland J. *The Parables of Jesus: A Commentary.* Grand Rapids, MI: Eerdmans, 2000.

Hunter, James Davison. *Culture Wars: The Struggle to Define America.* New York: HarperCollins, 1991.

Hutchinson, William R. *The Modernist Impulse in American Protestantism.* New York: Oxford University Press, 1976, 1982.

IRD = Institute on Religion and Democracy's "Reforming America's Churches Project 2001–2004" [no author, no date].

GNA = "Issues and Priorities: General Conference 2004," *Good News Agenda* [no author, no date].

Jackson, Glenna S., "The Complete Gospel: Jesus and Women via the Jesus Seminar." *Feminist Theology* 28 (2001): 27–39.

Jackson, Glenna S. "Jesus as First-Century Feminist: Christian Anti-Judaism?" *Feminist Theology* 19 (1998): 85–98.

Jaspers, Karl, and Rudolf Bultmann. *Myth and Christianity. An Inquiry into the Possibility of Religion without Myth.* Trans. Norbert Guterman. New York: Noonday Press, 1958.

Kaufman, Gordon D. *In Face of Mystery: A Constructive Theology.* Cambridge, MA: Harvard University Press, 1993.

Kaufman, Gordon D. *Theology in a Nuclear Age.* Louisville: Westminster John Knox Press, 1985.

Kloppenborg Verbin, John. *Excavating Q: The History and Setting of the Sayings Gospel.* Minneapolis: Fortress Press, 2000.

Koester, Helmut. "Writings and the Spirit: Authority and Politics in Ancient Christianity." *Harvard Theological Review* 84 (1991): 353–72.

Kristeva, Julia. *New Maladies of the Soul.* New York: Columbia University Press, 1995.

Lee, A. D. *Pagans and Christians in Late Antiquity. A Source Book.* London: Routledge, 2000.

Lemaire, André. "Earliest Archeological Evidence of Jesus found in Jerusalem," *Biblical Archaeology Review* 28.6 (November/December 2002): 24–33, 70.

Littell, Franklin H. "The Churches and the Body Politic." *Religion in America.* Eds. William McLoughlin and Robert Bellah. Boston: Beacon Press, 1966.

Littell, Franklin H. *From State Church to Pluralism: A Protestant Interpretation of Religion in American History.* Garden City, NY: Doubleday & Company, 1962.

Luedemann, Gerd. *The Resurrection of Jesus.* Minneapolis: Fortress Press, 1994.

Mack, Burton. *The Lost Gospel: The Book of Q and Christian Origins.* San Francisco: HarperSanFrancisco, 1994.

McDonald, Lee M. *The Formation of the Christian Biblical Canon.* Revised ed. Peabody, MA: Hendrickson, 1995.

McFague, Sallie. *Models of God: Theology for an Ecological, Nuclear Age.* Philadelphia: Fortress Press, 1987.

Meares, Ainslie. *From the Quiet Place—Mental Ataraxis Thoughts on Meditation.* Melbourne: Hill of Content, 1976.

Thomas Merton: Spiritual Master: The Essential Writings. Ed. Lawrence S. Cunningham. New York: Paulist Press, 1992.

Minear, Paul S. *The Bible and the Historian. Breaking the Silence About God in Biblical Studies.* Nashville: Abingdon Press, 2002.

Mudge, Lewis. *The Sense of a People: Toward a Church for the Human Future.* Philadelphia: Trinity Press International, 1992.

Murray, Bridget. "Same Office, Different Aspirations." *Monitor on Psychology* 32,11 (December 2001).

Mwombeki, Fidon R. "Reading the Bible in Contemporary Africa." *Word & World* 21,2 (2001): 121–28.

Nerney, Catherine and Hal Taussig. *Re-Imagining Life Together in America: A New Gospel of Community.* Lanham, MD: Sheed & Ward/Rowman & Littlefield, 2002.

Niebuhr, Reinhold. "Can Schweitzer Save Us from Russell?" *The Christian Century* (Sept. 3, 1925) 1094–95, as cited by Richard Wightman Fox, *Reinhold Niebuhr: A Biography.* New York: Pantheon, 1985.

Niebuhr, H. Richard. *Christ and Culture.* New York: Harper and Brothers, 1951.

Niebuhr, Reinhold. *Faith and History. A Comparison of Christian and Modern Views of History.* New York: Charles Scribner's Sons, 1949.

Niebuhr, Reinhold. *An Interpretation of Christian Ethics.* San Francisco: Harper & Row, 1935, 1963.

Niebuhr, Reinhold. *The Nature and Destiny of Man. A Christian Interpretation.* Vol. 2: *Human Destiny.* New York: Charles Scribner's Sons, 1943.

Nietzsche, F. *Thus Spake Zarathustra.* New York: Walter Kaufmann, 1978.

Patterson, Stephen J. *The God of Jesus: The Historical Jesus and the Search for Meaning.* Harrisburg, PA: Trinity Press International, 1998.

Pelikan, Jaroslav. *Bach Among the Theologians.* Philadelphia: Fortress Press, 1986.

Prelinger, Elizabeth et al. *After the Scream: The Late Paintings of Edvard Munch.*
New Haven: Yale University Press, 2002.

Pui-lan, Kwok. "Jesus/The Native: Biblical Studies from a Postcolonial
Perspective." *Teaching the Bible: The Discourses and Politics of Biblical Pedagogy.*
Eds. Fernando F. Segovia and Mary Ann Tolbert. Maryknoll, N.Y.: Orbis Books,
1998..

Putnam, Robert. *Bowling Alone: The Collapse and Revival of American Community.*
New York: Simon and Schuster, 2000.

Robinson, John A. T. *Honest to God.* Philadelphia: Westminster, 1963.

Rorty, Richard. *Philosophy and the Mirror of Nature.* Princeton, NJ: Princeton
University Press, 1979.

Ross, Owen K. "The Main Reasons for a New Approach To Do Theology in
Africa." Mutare, Zimbabwe: Africa University class paper, 2000.

Schweitzer, Albert.*The Quest of the Historical Jesus. A Critical Study of its Progress
from Reimarus to Wrede.* Trans. W. Montgomery. New York: Macmillan, 1968
(First ed. 1906).

Scott, Bernard Brandon. *Hear Then the Parable: A Commentary on the Parables of
Jesus.* Minneapolis: Fortress Press, 1989.

Scott, Bernard Brandon. *Re-Imagine the World: An Introduction to the Parables of
Jesus.* Santa Rosa, CA: Polebridge Press, 2001.

Shanks, Hershel. "The Storm over the Bone Box." *Biblical Archaeology Review* 29.5
(September/October 2003): 26–39, 83.

Simm, Laura. *Body and Soul* (January / February 2003): 53.

Soards, Marion L. "Paul." *Mercer Dictionary of the Bible.* Eds. Watson E. Mills, et
al. Macon, GA: Mercer University Press, 1990.

Sobel, Dava. *Galileo's Daughter. A Historical Memoir of Science, Faith, and Love.*
New York: Penguin Books, 2000.

Stevens, Wallace. "Cy est pourtraicte, madam ste Ursule, et les unze mille vierges."
The Collected Poems of Wallace Stevens. New York: Alfred A. Knopf, 1961.

Tarnas, Richard. *The Passion of the Western Mind: Understanding the Ideas that Have
Shaped Our World View.* New York: Ballantine Books, 1993.

Taussig, Hal. *Jesus Before God: The Prayer Life of the Historical Jesus.* Santa Rosa,
CA: Polebridge Press, 1999.

Thich Nhat Hanh, *A Guide to Walking Meditation.* New Haven, CT: Eastern Press,
1985.

Tillich, Paul. *Systematic Theology.* 3 vols. Chicago: University of Chicago Press,
1951–1963.

Volf, Miroslav. "Way of Life." *The Christian Century* (November 20–December 3,
2002): 35.

Weaver, Walter P. *The Historical Jesus in the Twentieth Century 1900–1950.*
Harrisburg, PA.: Trinity Press International, 1999.

West, Morris. *A View from the Bridge.* Sydney: HarperCollins, 1996.

Wilber, K., *The Marriage of Sense and Soul.* Melbourne: Hill of Content, 1998.

Wire, Antoinette. *The Corinthian Women Prophets.* Philadelphia: Fortress Press,
1983.

Wuthnow, Robert. *Loose Connections: Joining Together in America's Fragmented
Communities.* Cambridge: Harvard University Press, 1998.

Young, R. "Fundamentalism as Terrorism." *Free Associations* 49 (2000): 26.